ENHANCING
ORGANIZATIONAL
PERFORMANCE

D1608633

ENHANCING
ORGANIZATIONAL
PERFORMANCE

A TOOLBOX FOR SELF-ASSESSMENT

Charles Lusthaus, Marie-Hélène Adrien,
Gary Anderson, and Fred Carden

INTERNATIONAL DEVELOPMENT RESEARCH CENTRE
Ottawa • Cairo • Dakar • Johannesburg • Montevideo • Nairobi • New Delhi • Singapore

Published by the International Development Research Centre
PO Box 8500, Ottawa, ON, Canada K1G 3H9

Canadian Cataloguing in Publication Data
Main entry under title:
Enhancing organizational performance : a toolbox for self-assessment
Issued also in French under title : Améliorer la performance organisationnelle.
ISBN 0-88936-870-8

1.	Organizational effectiveness — Handbooks, guides, etc.
2.	Sustainable development — Developing countries.
I.	Lusthaus, Charles.
II.	International Developemnet Resarch Centre (Canada)

HD58.9E6 1998   658.1   C99-980037-X

IDRC Books endeavours to produce environmentally friendly publications. All paper used is recycled as well as recyclable. All inks and coatings are vegetable-based products.

CONTENTS

Foreword ix

Preface xi

How to use this guide xiii

CHAPTER 1 – SHOULD YOU CONDUCT A SELF-ASSESSMENT? 1
Why would you conduct a self-assessment? 1
    Some typical reasons for conducting a self-assessment 2
    Exercise 1. Identifying the reasons 3
Are you ready? 3
    Exercise 2. Getting ready 5
    Stop or go? 6
How long will it take? 6
Before you begin 7
Who will use the results? 7
    Stakholders 8
    Exercise 3. Mapping the stakeholders 9
Who should conduct the process? 10
    Creating a team 11
    Who will do what? 11
    What does your team have? What does your team need? 12
    Are there any other roles or responsibilities? 12
    Exercise 4. Building the team 13
What's the best way to manage the process? 14
What issues may arise at preplanning? 14
Have you forgotten anything? 16

CHAPTER 2 – PLANNING A SELF-ASSESSMENT 17
What is the unit of analysis? 18
What are the main performance issues? 18
    Exercise 5. Identifying preliminary performance 20
What are the right questions? 20
    Three kinds of question 21
    Prioritizing your set of questions 21
What are the indicators? 22
    A few words of caution about indicators 23
    Exercise 6. Developing indicators 25
What are the best sources of data? 25
What methods will be used to collect data? 26
    Exercise 7. Selecting methodologies 31
    Exercise 8. Completing the self-assessment matrix 32
Have you forgotten anything? 32

CHAPTER 3 – CONDUCTING A SELF-ASSESSMENT 33

Planning for data collection 33

Collecting the data 34

Analyzing your data 35

      Data sources and triangulation...36

      Sorting the data 37

      Basis for judgment 38

Communicating the results 38

      Communicating during the process 39

      Communicating after the process...39

      Hints for conveying results..39

      Writing a good report 40

What issues may arise at this stage? 40

How will the results be used? 42

      Why results get shelved 43

**CHAPTER 4 – DIAGNOSING THE PERFORMANCE
OF YOUR ORGANIZATION** 45

A framework for assessing organizational performance.....................45

Organizational performance 46

      Effectiveness 47

      Efficiency 48

      Relevance 49

      Financial viability 50

      Exercise 9. *Analyzing organizational performance* 51

External environment 52

      Administrative and legal environment..53

      Political environment..53

      Sociocultural environment 54

      Economic environment...54

      Technological environment 55

      Stakeholder environment 55

      Exercise 10. *Understanding the organization's external environment* 56

Organizational motivation 57

      History 58

      Mission: stated and perceived 58

      Culture 59

      Incentives 60

      Exercise 11. *Determining organizational motivation*....................60

Organizational capacity 61
    Strategic leadership 62
    Human resources 66
    Financial management..70
    Infrastructure..72
    Program management...75
    Organizational processes..77
    Interinstitutional linkages 80
    Exercise 12. Examining organizational capacity 82
    Exercise 13. Summarizing the performance issues......................83

APPENDIX 1 – Tools for self-assessment.................................85
Tool 1. The five-easy-pieces model for a quick self-assessment.........85
Tool 2. Stakeholder assessment 86
Tool 3. Performance-issues worksheet 88
Tool 4. Culture audit..89
Tool 5. Work breakdown 90
Tool 6. Person–day analysis 92

APPENDIX 2 – Tips for designing data-collection instruments...............93
Tip 1. Group techniques...94
Tip 2. Interviews 99
Tip 3. Questionnaires 103
Tip 4. Basis for judgment 112

APPENDIX 3 – Sample questionnaires......................................113
Sample 1. Staff questionnaire 113
Sample 2. Donor questionnaire 117
Sample 3. Cover letter for donor questionnaire 119

APPENDIX 4 – Sample self-assessment exercises....................121
*Exercise A1. Who is XYZ? What are the strengths and weaknesses
   of our internal environment?*..122
Exercise A2. Our external context 124
Exercise A3. Dreaming about the future...125
Exercise A4. Beginning to bridge the gaps..126

The authors..127

Contacting us 128

FOREWORD

Since the International Development Research Centre (IDRC) was founded in 1970, it has funded research aimed at solving development problems. Our programs are driven by the conviction that sustainable development is possible only if people have the knowledge they need to secure their own well-being. IDRC has chosen to contribute to this goal by strengthening the research capacity of individuals and institutions in the South.

Capacity-building for individual researchers is relatively straightforward. Like many agencies, we at IDRC have learned to provide opportunities for training, collaboration with other researchers, and research-project funding, with considerable success. By comparison, donor agencies appear to be less clear about how to build capacity within institutions and organizations. Over the past few years, IDRC has increased its efforts to learn more about what makes research institutions effective and viable.

In 1995, we published *Institutional Assessment: A Framework for Strengthening Organizational Capacity for IDRC's Research Partners*. This publication was translated as *Évaluation institutionelle* in 1996. These books were the product of collaboration between IDRC's Evaluation Unit and Universalia Management Group (a Canadian management consulting firm). These books identified and brought together a series of questions on an organization's external environment, its motivation, its internal capacity, and its performance. This series of questions was intended as a practical guide for assessing an organization's ability to sustain itself and to meet its goals.

Working with Universalia, we field-tested the framework with IDRC's Southern partners. We wanted to find out whether it could help diagnose an organization's strengths and weaknesses, guide an organization in formulating a capacity-building response, and assist in assessing the outcome of an intervention. Our partners responded positively to the framework and contributed their own ideas about how it might be refined and used. Two important themes emerged from the field tests: organizations often prefer to assess themselves, rather than employ external evaluators; and organizations unprepared to conduct a full-scale assessment often wish to conduct a smaller, problem-based exercise focusing on a specific area or situation. This book is a response to these needs. It is a self-assessment guide with flexible tools and techniques that can be adapted and used severally or together.

Having received enthusiastic responses to our assessment framework, we are excited about this publication. We sincerely hope that it will open new possibilities for organizations to improve their performance and sustain their programs and that it will provide the basis for improved, more effective relationships between funding and recipient organizations.

This guidebook is a work in progress, and so we look forward to receiving your comments and suggestions on improving it. You can reach us at the addresses noted at the back of the book ("Contacting us"). Your comments will be valued and will enrich our work.

Taken together, *Institutional Assessment*, *Évaluation institutionelle*, and this book, *Enhancing Organizational Performance*, are designed to assist IDRC and its partners in creating and maintaining organizations well-adapted to serving the needs of the world's poor.

Terry Smutylo
Director, Evaluation
International Development Research Centre

PREFACE

Organizations usually conduct self-assessments to better understand their own performance and to address their strategic issues and thus, ultimately, to improve their performance. Organizational self-assessment is often used as a diagnostic, or a starting point, for organizations implementing an internal change or strategic planning process, or both. It can also be used as a way to engage in dialogue with other stakeholders, such as the Board of Directors or donor agencies.

Enhancing Organizational Performance was developed to accompany our previous publications, *Institutional Assessment* and *Évaluation institutionnelle*, which described our conceptual framework for assessing organizational capacity through various possible interventions, such as internal self-assessments or external evaluations by a funding agency.

Our model of self-assessment goes beyond measuring the results of an organization's programs, products, and services. It integrates these results with the techniques of formative assessment, in which the assessment team becomes involved in helping the organization become more effective in meeting its goals. Focusing on organizational self-assessment, the framework has since been tested in a variety of organizations around the world.

This guide is not definitive. It has evolved as organizations share their experiences with us. As a matter of interest, if you are familiar with our book *Institutional Assessment*, you will notice that in this guide we have refined or expanded some of the terms used in our original model. This is a true sign of work in progress. We invite you to share your experiences and comments on this guide and the self-assessment process it presents.

We wish to thank the International Development Research Centre's (IDRC's) Evaluation Unit, whose preoccupation with providing support to the Centre in building research capacity led to the development of this framework and its testing in the field. We would especially like to thank Terry Smutylo and Cerstin Sander, who reviewed and improved the final drafts of this guide. We are also indebted to the IDRC program officers who identified the contexts in which we could work and who worked with us in many different ways to improve the model. IDRC's strong and constructive linkages with its partner institutions made it possible to test the approach so effectively.

Most especially we would like to thank the staff and leaders of the organizations with which we worked. It was a privilege and an opportunity to work with

Dr Soekartawi of the Southeast Asia Ministers of Education Organization (Philippines); Dr Souleymane Soulama of the Centre d'études, de documentation, de recherches économiques et sociales, Burkina Faso; Dr Tade Aina, Dr Mkandawire Thandika, and Dr Achille Mbembe of the Council for the Development of Social Science Research in Africa, Senegal; Mr A.V.S. Reddy of the Centre for Integrated Rural Development for Asia and the Pacific (CIRDAP), Bangladesh; Dr Joseph Yao Yao and Dr Aïssata Camara of the Centre ivoirien de recherches économiques et sociales, Côte d'Ivoire; Dr Diagne Abdoulaye of the Centre de recherches économiques appliquées, Senegal.

We extend special thanks to Ms Rosalie Y. Say, Head of Training at CIRDAP, for her valuable contributions to the final draft of this guide; to Ms Julie Valentine, researcher; and to Ms Carroll Salomon, our editor.

Charles Lusthaus
Universalia Management Group

HOW TO USE THIS GUIDE

This guide and the self-assessment process it presents can be used in a variety of ways. Our main objective was to provide you with a process for conducting an assessment, a framework for assessing issues, and some tools and tips to help you as you address an issue – big or small – that your organization is facing.

The guide is divided into four chapters and four appendixes. The first three chapters describe the major elements of the self-assessment process. The fourth chapter reviews the performance framework developed by Universalia Management Group and the International Development Research Centre and provides checklists and exercises to help you diagnose organizational-performance issues. Appendix 1 contains samples of self-assessment tools that some organizations have found useful in the self-assessment process, and Appendix 2 concerns the design of data-collection instruments. These tools and tips are referred to throughout the text, identified by a ![icon]. We hope you will copy or adapt some or all of these tools to help you in your own self-assessment process and let us know what you think of them. Throughout the guide, we have included short stories or anecdotes about our experiences with self-assessment that we hope will bring you a sense of how this process works, as well as exercises, marked by a ![icon] to help with various parts of the process. Appendix 3 contains sample questionnaires. In Appendix 4 you will find some sample self-assessment exercises.

In our work, some organizations used parts of this guide to address a set of organizational questions that managers often ask themselves: What business are we in? Are we having an impact on our client group? Are people happy in our organization? These organizations used the framework and some of the tools and managed to find problem-solving time in their regular meetings.

Other organizations, undergoing more dramatic shifts, opted for a more thorough review. They used the approach presented in this guide in a more systematic way and allocated special time and resources to undergo the self-assessment process. You are the best judge of how you can make the guide useful to your own organization.

USING THE SELF-ASSESSMENT APPROACH

In this guide and in our work, the term *self-assessment* refers to an approach to organizational diagnosis in which the organization has some measure of control over the assessment. The degrees of control range from assessments controlled entirely by the organization to those commissioned by an entity external to the organization but in which the organization fully participates and owns the results. The control of the process appears at different points on this continuum in the experiences described in this guide.

Although we have described the self-assessment process in a certain sequence in this guide, we do not intend to suggest that all self-assessments follow these steps rigidly or in this order. Many organizations engage in self-assessment at different stages or in a unique framework that makes the best sense for a given organization. Sometimes an organization seeks an overview of its operations; at other times, it may have a specific problem to address, and a full-blown institutional assessment would only get in the way. These two approaches to self-assessment appear graphically in Figure 1.

FIGURE 1. APPROACHES TO SELF-ASSESSMENT: THE ORGANIZATIONAL OVERVIEW AND THE ORGANIZATIONAL PROBLEM

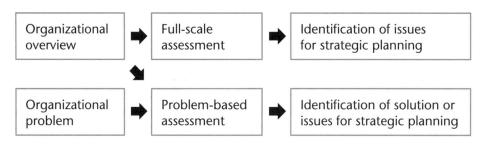

At a recent meeting and discussion with one partner, we even worked out a quick-assessment model.

SEE TOOL 1 – Quick-Assessment Model

See Tool 1 (the five-easy-pieces model for a quick self-assessment) in Appendix 1 (p. 85).

Before beginning, it is important to determine the objective of the exercise and to clarify the needs of the participants. By understanding and exploring your concerns and this approach, you will identify the ways you can reorganize it to best suit the needs and skills of your participants.

C H A P T E R 1

Should You Conduct a Self-Assessment?

. . . .

Before starting a self-assessment, you will need to make many decisions. You will need to ask some questions: Why are we doing this? How will we do it? Who will do it? In this chapter, we discuss

- Reasons for undertaking a self-assessment;
- Your organization's readiness for self-assessment;
- The users of the results and the interests of different stakeholders in the process;
- The scope of the intervention and required resources; and
- The self-assessment team.

WHY WOULD YOU CONDUCT A SELF-ASSESSMENT?

It is important to clarify your reasons for undertaking the self-assessment. Once you are clear about this, you will find it easier to determine

- The scope of the intervention;
- The depth of data required;
- Its focus in terms of issues (such as performance, capacity, organizational motivation, environment); and
- The cost.

Some typical reasons for conducting a self-assessment

It is common for an organization to conduct a self-assessment when it is at a turning point in its history. An organization may also find a self-assessment useful when it needs to make decisions about particular aspects of the organization itself:

- *Strategic decisions* – Should the organization grow? Merge? Shrink? Change its mission?
- *Program decisions* – Should programs be expanded? Should two or several programs be integrated? Should new services be offered?
- *Financial-feasibility decisions* – Should new investors be sought? Should funding sources be more diversified and how? Should new approaches to fundraising be identified?
- *Staffing decisions* – Should staff with different skills be hired to support the mission? Should the organization let some staff go, and if so, who?

Other reasons might be less specific; for example, the self-assessment might have the following objectives:

- To identify the organization's strengths and weaknesses – a first step toward improvement;
- To identify issues and problems before correction becomes difficult or impossible;
- To identify the needs that should be addressed through specific action;
- To identify human and other resources the organization can use to effectively improve its performance;
- To document the desired outcomes of the organization's activities;
- To generate information useful in planning and decision-making;
- To assist in fundraising; and
- To provide donors and other stakeholders with information about the organization's performance.

DEALING WITH FUNDING CUTS

The agency's major source of funding was to be cut within 9 months. The agency had to decide whether it should close down, cut down on staff and programs, or privatize. Each option had major implications for the agency's programs and services, staffing requirements, and funding mechanisms. To gain an understanding of these implications, the agencyundertook a self-assessment. With this knowledge, the organization was able to make an informed decision.

ORGANIZATIONAL CHANGE

The centre had never carried out a comprehensive review of its strengths and weaknesses, although it had conducted numerous project and program evaluations. The need for an in-depth organizational review was triggered by
- The arrival of a new executive director;
- Increased pressure on the organization to identify alternative funding sources; and
- The organization's desire to respond to the changing needs of its member institutions.

The process was also supported by one of its funders, who saw this approach as a way to build the capacities of the research centre.

EXERCISE 1. Identifying the reasons

Instructions: The following exercise can help members of your organization understand why they would conduct a self-assessment. Ask senior managers and other individuals or groups you think should be involved to reflect on this question and begin a list of their reasons for self-assessment. Their ideas can be shared and can become the basis for future decision-making. This exercise may be conducted on an individual basis, with the information then collated by one person, or it may be carried out as a group exercise, facilitated by either an internal or an external person.

In your organization, identify the three main reasons for undertaking a self-assessment at this time.

1. _____

    _____

2. _____

    _____

3. _____

    _____

ARE YOU READY?

Organizations need to have a certain degree of readiness to engage in self-assessment. Although there is no set number of variables to assess, you will want to consider some readiness concepts before beginning the process:
- *Cultural readiness* – This means that your organization has an organizational culture in which it is acceptable to provide suggestions for improvement.
- *Leadership readiness* – This means that leaders support the self-assessment and the allocation of resources to the process.

- *Resource readiness* – This means that you are prepared to commit the resources (people, time, money, and technology) needed to conduct the self-assessment. Although the type and amount of resources you will need to undertake the assessment will not be known until you begin, management's commitment to making the necessary resources available is indicated. Institutional self-assessments require more time from internal staff than externally conducted assessments do and typically involve more of the people on staff as well. This must be both understood and accepted. The assessment can have long-term benefits in terms of ownership and pace of implementation of change, but these will not be clear at the outset.
- *Vision and strategy readiness* – This means the organization has a sense of where it is going and how it should get there or has a desire to create a clearer vision.
- *People readiness* – This means the organization has people on staff who will champion the self-assessment process and be willing to work together through a process that may sometimes be ambiguous and will constantly be changing.
- *Systemic readiness* – This means the organization has or wants to have systems in place to provide the information needed to complete the data collection and support the self-assessment.

FACTORS THAT CAN AFFECT READINESS

You must have
- Acceptance of the process by leaders in the organization
- A champion
- Adequate internal resources (time and people) to do the self-assessment
- A compelling reason for doing the self-assessment

These are mixed blessings
- Other changes going on at the same time, some of which you cannot control
- An organization with a history of change
- Past experience with evaluations (positive or negative)

It's nice to have
- Leaders with credibility
- A clear vision in the organization of where it wants to go
- Additional resources (financial) to conduct the self-assessment

These can be major barriers
- Past failures and frustrations with self-assessment
- Superficial motives
- Low levels of skills and capabilities
- Negative incentives for self-assessment

EXERCISE 2. Getting ready

Instructions: This exercise will help you to decide whether you are ready to engage in a self-assessment. Ask a group of managers in your organization to reflect individually on these questions. Then use the list as a tool to collectively discuss the organization's readiness. There are no clear-cut answers to these questions. Your group will need to reach consensus on whether to proceed with the assessment.

Readiness assessment

1   To what extent do the senior leaders in your organization support the change process? Do staff have confidence in the leaders' ability to engage in change management?

2. To what extent is any individual (professional or manager) willing to champion the process and capable of doing so?

3. Is the organization facing the need to make strategic decisions and would a self-assessment help in the decision-making?

4. Does the organization have a clear vision of where it wishes to go?

5. Are major changes already going on within the organization that might slow down the process or interfere with it?

6. Does the organization have access to resources to carry out the process?

7. When was the last major organizational change? To what extent was it successful? Did it energize the staff or lower their morale?

8. Do people inside the organization have adequate skills to undertake this process?

9. To what extent are the leaders and staff comfortable with the use of organizational data? To what extent do organizational data exist?

10. Is this a good time for change? Would another time be better? Are there future incentives for change to occur now?

11. What are the positive, negative, neutral, or cultural implications of changing? Are people in your organization supported if they try new things?

Stop or go?

It is impossible to be absolutely sure that your organization is ready for a self-assessment. The readiness diagnosis will be based on your best judgment. The purpose of this diagnosis is not to achieve a definitive answer but to consider the elements that will contribute to a successful assessment process. Conditions change, and factors may lead to a revised *stop* or *go* at various stages in the process.

At this stage in the process, some organizations may, for a variety of reasons, decide that they do not want to proceed – because they are not fully ready, or they wish to begin the process at some later date. It is important to recognize this and not engage in the process without support from inside the organization.

HOW LONG WILL IT TAKE?

A self-assessment is a commitment of time and energy. It should provide you with knowledge of how to improve the performance of your organization. However, it is difficult to estimate how long it should take, as the process depends on many variables: the number of strategic issues you wish to explore, the scope of those issues, the type of data you need and their accessibility, availability of staff to be involved in the process, and the type of report you expect to present. These factors will affect the duration of the process.

The depth of data collection also depends on the quantity of information you need to understand an issue. This may not be obvious at the planning stage. As you begin to collect data on an issue, you may identify the need for more information. The deeper you go, the more you are led to uncover. The process will need to be guided by considerations of time, resources, availability of new data, and the importance of the issue.

One of the most critical elements affecting the scope of a self-assessment is the way your team will have to present its findings. It is quite time-consuming, for example, to produce a highly detailed report that links each finding to numerous data sources. This may or may not be necessary, depending on the audience and its expectations.

Understanding your audience will help you decide on the type of reporting required and the appropriate level of language. If the self-assessment is primarily for internal use, for example, then your report may comprise a set of brief notes, a summary of main lessons, or simply a memo. If, on the other hand, you have to inform external stakeholders of the results, you will need to discuss with them the way they wish to be informed (see "Communicating the results" in Chapter 3, p. 38). Remember, you can conduct a thoroughly professional but less formal process to support findings. You and your organization will need to weigh how much you will or can invest in the process.

In our experience, some organizations carried out the process in 12 months; others, with a focus on specific issues for internal use only, completed the assessment in 1 month.

Finally, specialized activities in the self-assessment can be delegated to produce certain data. For example, a financial analysis can be completed by your organization's accounting department, which can generate both the raw data and the graphics required to interpret them. Other elements can be contracted out. There are many options that you can use and control.

BEFORE YOU BEGIN

If your organization decides to engage in a self-assessment, you will have to do a number of things before carrying out the diagnosis. At this stage, you will probably want to

- Identify the users of the end results of the diagnosis;
- Clarify how the users wish to be informed about the results;
- Decide who should lead the self-assessment; and
- Decide how much time and effort will be allocated.

WHO WILL USE THE RESULTS?

The audience for the assessment will influence its scope and the types of result expected. The sooner you identify the final audience, the easier it will be to identify their needs. You will need to consult with the audience throughout the process to obtain a richer set of data:

- *Inside the organization* – The Board of Directors and senior officials use the results of organizational assessments to support their efforts in strategic management or organizational change. Professionals and staff may use assessment results to improve decisions related to their roles and responsibilities.
- *Outside the organization* – Funders and other organizational investors use organizational assessments to support internal change (learning)

efforts and to better understand the effects of their investments on the organization. Similarly, client groups and beneficiaries can use the results to better understand their relationship with the organization.

Stakeholders

Stakeholders are individuals or organizations that will be affected in some significant way by the outcome of the self-assessment process or that are affected by the performance of the organization, or both. As shown in Figure 2, most organizations have a wide range of stakeholders, some more influential than others (either because they benefit from the organization, they fund some of its activities, or there are political reasons). Not all stakeholders have the same stake in the organization, and it is important to recognize the level of influence each stakeholder has on your organization. This will guide the data-collection process and allow you to identify the main sources of data.

FIGURE 2. IDENTIFIED STAKEHOLDERS

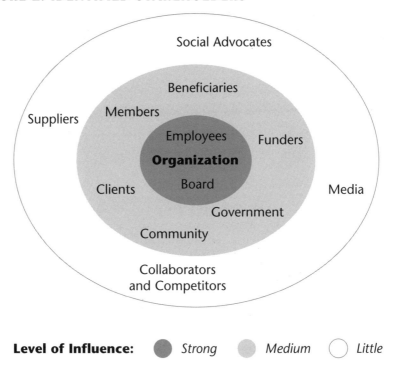

 SEE TOOL 2 – Stakeholder Assessment

See Tool 2 (stakeholder assessment) in Appendix 1 (p. 86). This can help you answer significant questions about your organization's stakeholders: Who are they? What do they want to know?

EXERCISE 3. Mapping the stakeholders

Instructions: Identify the various groups, in order of importance, with a stake or interest in your organization and the outcomes of the self-assessment. Write the names of these groups on Figure 3. The closer they are to the centre of the map, the greater their interest in, or influence on, your organization. When you have finished, complete the checklist for mapping stakeholders.

FIGURE 3. WHO ARE YOUR STAKEHOLDERS?

Checklist for mapping stakeholders

☐ Have all primary and secondary stakeholders been identified?

☐ Have all potential supporters and opponents of the organization been identified?

☐ Have all the other stakeholders that are likely to emerge as a result of the self-assessment been identified?

☐ Have stakeholders' interests been identified?

☐ Have stakeholders' interrelationships been identified?

☐ Have the self-assessment goals been reconciled with stakeholders' needs, interests, and priorities?

☐ Has stakeholder participation in the self-assessment been investigated?

WHO SHOULD CONDUCT THE PROCESS?

Part of the planning phase is to determine roles and responsibilities. At this stage, you can form a self-assessment team to guide the process. Self-assessment teams have two major roles: strategic and operational.

In some cases, you will need to have two separate teams; in other cases, one team with two distinct roles. Regardless of the structure, select team members carefully, according to the role to be fulfilled. The strategic role will require people to provide guidelines and directions for the process and will oversee its overall quality. The operational role will require people to be more involved in the data collection, analysis, and reporting. The skills required for these roles are quite different, and several factors will influence your selection of team members: their availability, the complexity of the assessment questions, and the purpose and scope of the self-assessment.

Although the same individuals may play both strategic and operational roles on a self-assessment team, it is important to recognize that certain responsibilities will be more important at some stages of the process and less important at others. The strategic responsibilities are more conceptual; the operational responsibilities, more hands-on.

The size of the self-assessment team will also be important. Enough people should be there to provide a range of views, but not so many that it becomes difficult to make decisions. How decisions will be made and who will make them should be agreed on early in the process and will depend on the types of decision to be made.

CONFIGURING A TEAM

An internal self-assessment team
In one case, the executive director drew up a self-assessment team comprising several young professionals and led by the head of training. The team was responsible for all aspects of the self-assessment process. Its work was reviewed by the executive director.

A combination of internal and external team members
In another organization, the self-assessment process was led by a team of two very senior managers, who contracted external consultants to carry out specific aspects of the process, such as data collection and analysis of some issues. The team then integrated these external reports into its own synthesis.

A steering committee to guide the self-assessment process
In a third organization, the senior managers operated as a steering committee responsible for the strategic aspects of the self-assessment. The managers mandated diverse individuals inside the organization to conduct elements of the process.

Creating a team

The following criteria can help in selecting team members likely to commit to the process and see it through:

- *Credibility* – Someone who is recognized by the main stakeholders and by members of the organization as having the appropriate mix of authority, responsibility, knowledge of the organization, and insight;
- *Technical expertise* – Someone who understands the self-assessment approach, can share responsibilities for the planning, management, and use of the self-assessment, is knowledgeable of the programs and services the organization offers, understands the organization and its issues, and can analyze data;
- *Impartiality* – Someone who can balance the perspectives of different people;
- *Communication skills* – Someone who can communicate the results of the self-assessment in a manner easily understood by all parties;
- *Interpersonal skills* – Someone who can interact with all parties in a sensitive and effective manner and is able to work on a team; and
- *Availability* – Someone who is available to conduct the self-assessment and will commit time to working on it.

Who will do what?

Self-assessment is an introspective process. Because the players are involved with the content of the assessment and have some stake in the organization, sensitivities can be strong. A clear definition of the roles and of the process at the outset can help ease tensions. Your organization needs to have a clear process for entering into a self-assessment, for managing the self-assessment, and for dealing with the expected and unexpected. On the other hand, self-assessment is not intended to be a scientific inquiry; rather, it is an organizational-development intervention and must be kept within the context of available resources.

Facilitation skills are important, to ensure voices are heard, to manage differences, and to create opportunities for consensus-building. The experience and knowledge of the team members enrich the self-assessment process. At the beginning, it is important to understand your team members' levels of skill and knowledge and what they need or want to learn. This information will help you make decisions about how the work of the team should be allocated.

What does your team have? What does your team need?

Some team members will have a deeper understanding of the organization and its issues; others will be able to provide comparative data from their experience in other organizations; and some will be more skilled in the self-assessment process. All of these skills and knowledge will be useful to the self-assessment.

Self-assessment is a learning process for all members. The team members you bring together are unlikely to have all the necessary skills for the self-assessment process. You will need to decide what skills or characteristics are most important, using the checklist below.

**CHECKLIST FOR SKILLS AND KNOWLEDGE
OF THE SELF-ASSESSMENT TEAM**

YES	NO	
☐	☐	Does the team have sufficient skills and knowledge about assessment techniques (how to conduct an interview, how to prioritize questions, where to look for data, how to analyze data, etc.)?
☐	☐	Does the team have sufficient skills and knowledge about the functioning of the organization?
☐	☐	Does the team have sufficient skills and knowledge about stakeholders' needs and the environment in which the organization operates?
☐	☐	Do team members have the time to devote to the self-assessment, in addition to that needed for their normal work?
☐	☐	Do team members have the facilitation skills required to conduct a self-assessment?

Are there any other roles or responsibilities?

In addition to the roles of the self-assessment team itself, the roles and responsibilities of other organizational members may need to be clarified. The Board of Directors, for example, may be required to participate in data collection or follow-up.

One should also consider the roles of external stakeholders – for example, external funders who support or partially support the self-assessment; and external professional consultants who may have been contracted to support part or all of the process.

The earlier the roles and responsibilities of these other players are defined, the easier it will be to proceed. To be effective, the process must be transparent, participatory, and empowering; above all, it must be a joint learning process. You may need to be creative about using local and external resources. You may want to consider outside resources to save time or to handle very sensitive issues.

HANDLING SENSITIVE ISSUES

Taking advantage of influential team members
In one organization, the executive director's role was voluntarily minimal during the self-assessment process. However, he did play a crucial role, ensuring that important stakeholders would provide needed data: he was quite influential and respected in his region, and he personally called stakeholders and encouraged them to respond to the questionnaire sent by the operational team. Needless to say, the response rate increased!

Gaining historical perspective
In one organization, in addition to the operational team and the management members, the self-assessment involved a former executive director (the founder of the centre), who was able to provide an historical perspective on many of the issues. This individual's role was invaluable.

EXERCISE 4. Building the team

Instructions: This exercise can help you think about the best combination of people to bring into your team. Consider the questions and then complete a grid like the one shown here.

1. In your organization, who will be on the team?

   _____

2. What value will they add to the team?

   _____

3. What roles are foreseen for them in the process?

Name	Special skills	Role

WHAT'S THE BEST WAY TO MANAGE THE PROCESS?

A self-assessment team brings together people for a short time. It is important for the team members to discuss the process and set rules for how they will operate.

QUESTIONS TO ASK ABOUT THE MANAGEMENT OF THE ASSESSMENT PROCESS	
Item	**Questions to ask**
Surface discussion	How will the team get beneath surface issues in discussions, particularly on sensitive issues?
Competition vs collaboration	How can the team promote a climate in which the members support rather than undercut each other?
Protection of confidentiality	How can the team see to it that all the information is made available to all team members and that confidentiality is maintained?
Freedom of expression	To what extent should team members be free to express feelings and opinions during the self-assessment process?
Wise use of resources	How will the team maximize the use of individual members and the combined resources of all the members?
Win–win conflict resolution	To what extent will the team confront emotional or intellectual conflicts? On what bases will conflicts be addressed?

WHAT ISSUES MAY ARISE AT PREPLANNING?

In a self-assessment, the goal is to present the positive aspects of the organization, as well as the problems that may have been unknown or unclear or that have not been addressed or talked about. The self-assessment process takes for granted a spirit of openness and a willingness to divulge vulnerabilities and to acknowledge and examine organizational strengths and weaknesses.

However, self-assessment is not necessarily a notion accepted in all cultures, and group discussion of the issues may be uncomfortable for people in some cultures or organizations. Fear of the unknown can create tension and sometimes resistance.

In our experiences with self-assessment with a variety of organizations, we found several recurring concerns or obstacles:

- Fear of change;
- Fear of the purposes for which the results are to be used;
- Difficulty securing senior-level participation and input;

- Procrastination, which is often due to a lack of clarity about roles and responsibilities;
- Lack of appropriate skill sets;
- Conflicts (difficulty understanding one another, conflicting work habits, conflicts among people who do not otherwise work together, conflicts in time allocation);
- Conflicts between project cycles and the organizational-assessment cycle; and
- Lack of communication, resulting in a distorted image of the project.

Although these problems have no simple solutions, it is important to consider how they could affect the self-assessment process. The team will need to manage conflict using an approach appropriate to the organization. Conflicts can often be prevented by holding regular dialogue sessions and by taking advantage of opportunities to engage people in the process, both formally and informally.

DEALING WITH CONFLICT

Acknowledging resistance
At one organization, a member of the self-assessment team had had a difficult experience in the past with an external self-assessment consultant. Because of that experience, the member initially showed a great deal of resistance to the process this time. The new consultant had to acknowledge and deal with this resistance before the self-assessment could actually move forward.

Clarifying required skill set
One institution had many researchers skilled in their own areas of research but less skilled in self-assessment. Although data collection, analysis, and communication of results are important in both research activities and self-assessment, they differ in important ways: in scope, design of instruments, and expectations of reliability. Until these differences were clarified, the self-assessment team faced a group of researchers who were very uncomfortable with being made responsible for the data-collection and data-analysis segments of the self-assessment. A consultant facilitated this process of clarification.

Resolving time conflicts
In one organization, the self-assessment was undertaken officially, and everyone was informed. In practice, however, the staff members responsible for the self-assessment did not have enough time to both conduct the assessment and continue their normal professional activities. Ultimately, the team asked management to resolve this issue.

HAVE YOU FORGOTTEN ANYTHING?

If you answer "no" to any of the questions below, review this chapter and complete the steps you need to get to "yes," before continuing with planning a self-assessment in Chapter 2.

REVIEW QUESTIONS

YES NO

☐ ☐ Are you clear about why your organization is going to conduct a self-assessment?

☐ ☐ Are you satisfied that your organization is ready to engage in a self-assessment process?

☐ ☐ Is your organization prepared to commit the appropriate financial and human resources to carry out the process?

☐ ☐ Are you clear about who the main audience is for the results of this process?

☐ ☐ Do you understand their expectations?

☐ ☐ Have you identified a team well suited to carrying out the self-assessment?

☐ ☐ Do you have a sense of the scope of the process you intend to undertake?

☐ ☐ Are the resources for this process adequate for collecting data with the level of credibility you wish to attain?

C H A P T E R   2

Planning a Self-Assessment

· ·

A self-assessment project requires some organizing to ensure that your team focuses on the right issues, uses its resources in the most efficient way throughout the process, and uses the appropriate instruments to collect and analyze the information.

You may find that developing a self-assessment matrix makes the task of organizing a self-assessment easier. Developing the matrix will help you

- Build on issues identified in assessing the need for self-assessment;
- Identify indicators that will help you answer the questions and subquestions you have about various organizational-performance issues;
- Identify sources of data to answer these questions; and
- Identify data-collection methods best suited to your questions and to your realities and constraints;

SAMPLE SELF-ASSESSMENT MATRIX					
Major issue	Key question	Subquestion	Indicators	Sources of data	Data-collection method

The following sections will guide you through the steps of creating a self-assessment matrix in detail. The steps are based on our framework for diagnosing organizational issues affecting the performance of an organization, developed in our earlier work, *Institutional Assessment*. If you are not familiar with the performance framework, you might want to read Chapter 4 before continuing. Chapter 4 provides a detailed breakdown of the areas of performance you may need to assess, as well as some sample questions.

As you begin the process of planning an assessment, you can expect to undertake some of the following activities:

- Identifying the unit of analysis for the self-assessment;
- Identifying the main performance issues to be addressed;
- Outlining a plan for conducting the self-assessment (including key questions, sources, and levels of effort); and
- Choosing methods to collect information and develop instruments (including indicators, data sources, and methods for data collection and analysis).

WHAT IS THE UNIT OF ANALYSIS?

Organizational assessments can be conducted at many levels. Your assessment may examine the entire organization, a department, or a work unit – these are all, in fact, organizational units you can assess. You must define the unit of analysis at the outset, as many of your subsequent decisions will depend on this decision.

WHAT ARE THE MAIN PERFORMANCE ISSUES?

One of your self-assessment team's first tasks will be to identify the most important issues affecting the organization – issues that the organization needs to resolve to improve its performance. These key issues will be the "strategic questions" of the self-assessment.

Typically, organizational issues centre around effectiveness (how well your organization is performing in achieving its mission), efficiency (how well it is using its resources to reach its mission), relevance (how well your organization's mission continues to serve the purpose of your various stakeholders), and financial viability (whether you have adequate funding to ensure that your organization can continue to perform in the short and long terms). You may identify issues in any or all of these areas. Many organizations tend to focus on effectiveness. Research institutions, for example, tend to focus on their research-and-publication issues, as these are the core of their business, their raison d'être. Nevertheless, you should consider all four performance areas.

The self-assessment team or committee will also need to prioritize the issues to decide the depth of analysis each one warrants. Although it is important for you to identify key strategic issues at the planning stage, it is equally important to recognize that issues will become more sharply focused as the process of self-assessment unfolds and that the balance of depth of analysis among the issues can change.

Even before you collect any systematic data, you will be able to find people in the organization with some notion of the performance issues it is facing. Senior leaders are a good source, and by asking them to help identify issues you build their sense of ownership of the process. However, everyone in the organization will have potentially useful views.

One approach to identifying the main issues is to ask several appropriate people inside the organization to reflect on issues they feel are important and to describe why they believe these are important issues. A few examples of issues and the reasons people gave for their concern are given below.

ISSUES AND REASONS FOR CONCERN

Major performance issues	Why these aspects of our performance are a concern
Are we fulfilling our mission adequately?	We are at a turning point in our organization's history, at which strategic decisions need to be made
Are we using our resources in the best way to fulfill our mission?	The organization is showing a decrease in its ability to fulfill its mission
Are our mission, programs, and services still relevant to those who benefit from them and those who support them?	Stakeholders (staff, funders, Board of Directors) express dissatisfaction with the organization
Are we financially viable or should we pursue additional sources of financing and funding?	

EXERCISE 5. Identifying preliminary performance issues

Instructions: We suggest you make several copies of this exercise and distribute them to your team members and the managers of the organization. Ask each person to complete the chart below. Then, as a group, you can compare and discuss your individual responses and "brainstorm" the priorities until you reach reasonable consensus on the main issues.

In the first column, fill in what you believe to be the major organizational-performance issues. In the second column, fill in some of the evidence or reasons you have for believing these are problems.

Main Performance Issue	What makes you think this is a problem?

WHAT ARE THE RIGHT QUESTIONS?

Once your team has identified the main performance issues, you will need to develop key questions about those issues to guide you in your data collection. A variety of approaches can be used to develop questions. This section suggests some starting points, but you can modify these to suit your needs and nature of your team.

Three kinds of questions

- *Descriptive questions* – Such questions require descriptive information about specific conditions or events. The answers describe what is happening now.
- *Normative questions* – Such questions require you to compare an observed outcome with an expected level of performance. The answers describe what should be done.
- *Impact questions* – Such questions require analyses of whether observed conditions or events can be attributed to program operations. The answers describe cause-and-effect relationships.

How you write the question will depend on what information you need to understand the issue. An example is given below.

SAMPLE QUESTIONS REGARDING EFFICIENT USE OF RESOURCES		
Issue	**Sample questions**	**Type of question**
Efficient use of resources	How were funds allocated this year?	Descriptive question
	Were funds disbursed according to standard budget procedures?	Normative question
	Was the planned budget appropriate to the needs of the organization?	Impact question

Prioritizing your set of questions

When the team is satisfied that it has developed a satisfactory set of questions on the issues, you will need to prioritize these questions according to the following factors:

- *Resource levels* – These are the people and time you have to invest in the self-assessment process. The more resources the organization has available, the more scope and depth the assessment can have. Eliminate questions you cannot afford to answer.
- *Purpose of the self-assessment* – Questions should be prioritized according to the overall purpose of the assessment. Eliminate questions that you do not need to answer.
- *Stakeholder's interests* – Some questions may be more important to one set of stakeholders than to others. Questions will need to reflect a balance of your stakeholders' needs.

WHAT ARE THE INDICATORS?

At this point in the development of your self-assessment matrix, the team will need to decide what type of answers it needs for each of the assessment questions – in other words, what type of information will satisfy the team? This is the time to develop indicators.

An indicator is a measuring device that allows you to clarify and measure a concept. Indicators make a concept more tangible, give you something to measure, and allow measuring to take place over time. They can help you clarify what it is you really want to know. As an example, we often ask about the size of an organization. Size is an important organizational concept, but it is also quite ambiguous. What is a good indicator of size?

- The number of staff?
- The number of clients served?
- The gross revenues?
- All of these?

The process of discussing and developing indicators can help team members reach a common understanding of what is being measured and why.

Indicators are used in a wide variety of contexts (such as those of planning, monitoring, and evaluation) and in all functional areas (such as those of finance, programing, and infrastructure). Indicators help you to describe organizational performance and the capacity, environment, and motivation driving organizational performance.

Indicators can be quantitative or qualitative. The difference between quantitative and qualitative indicators is sometimes subtle, and they are sometimes mixed together. In general, quantitative indicators are numeric representations of a concept (for example, the number of refereed research articles written as a result of a project). Qualitative indicators are less tangible. They are often an individual's perceptions of a situation and are not always easy to count (for example, descriptions of the ways people found the research useful).

Indicators are also either direct or indirect. A direct indicator measures the concept itself – if you want to know staff size, for example, you count the number of staff. Indirect indicators measure something that happens as a result of the concept.

AN INDIRECT BUT APPROPRIATE INDICATOR

Some researchers were studying access to clean water in a rural region in Africa. They found that the most reliable indicator of a village's access to clean water was the school attendance of the girls in the village!

Well, in that region, young girls were sent to collect water for the family. If the only clean water was far from the village, the girls had no time to attend school. Therefore, the more young girls in class, the more likely it would be that village had ready access to clean water.

Indicators may be general or specific: they may work in any situation at any time (for example, staff size), or they may need to be adjusted to a particular context (as demonstrated in the questions about size, listed above). Also, even in a particular context, indicators can be transitory, even seasonal.

INDICATORS MATURE WITH THE ORGANIZATION

In one organization, the executive director made an interesting link between the age of the organization and the level of sophistication of its indicators:

"When we began," she said, "all we cared about was staying afloat, and our main indicator was having enough money to run our programs. After a few years, we began to serve a broader clientele and started monitoring whether they liked our services (we introduced a client-satisfaction survey). It wasn't until a few years ago that we started worrying about the costs of treating each client and the increase or decrease of funds from each funder."

A few words of caution about indicators

To identify indicators well, you have to develop a clear picture of what you are trying to measure – indicators shouldn't be the starting point – and even then there are a few other things you need to be careful about.

First, indicators often express the values of the people who develop them. The ways one measures a concept can give that concept importance in an organization and can even change organizational activities, for better or for worse. If, for example, a research institution or university rates researchers or professors on the number of experiments they conduct or articles they write, someone might perceive this as encouraging quantity rather than quality of research. Or, if a funding agency decides that the relevance of a particular social-service agency should be measured by the number of people it serves in the community, this might lead to a reduction in the time spent with each person.

Second, it is sometimes difficult to develop adequate indicators to measure the complex dynamics in organizations – often indicators are too simplistic and need to be combined. Most organizations develop a set of carefully considered indicators and modify them over time as they analyze their results.

Third, indicators may sometimes point out an organizational paradox or contradiction; that is, they give conflicting signals for the same concept. For example, diversification of funding could be seen as both a positive indicator and a negative indicator. On the one hand, it is a sign that an organization is financially viable and not overly reliant on one donor. On the other hand, having several donors (each with its own evaluation frameworks, indicators, and expectations) can lead to fragmented program vision and evaluation requirements, which can make it more difficult to develop coherent programs.

In all the organizations we worked with, the most difficult part of the diagnosis was identifying indicators. Sometimes this was because of an abundance of indicators and the difficulty of finding ones that really mattered. In one case, described below, there was another, far more interesting reason.

INDICATORS CAN LEAD YOU IN DIFFERENT DIRECTIONS

One regional centre had received funding to develop a resource centre (library) to serve the region. This gave rise to debates about the best indicators to measure performance. Some wanted to measure inputs, such as the number of new books acquired and new computers installed. However, given the centre's mandate to promote regional cooperation and to support local government, others wanted more output-oriented indicators, such as the increase in the number of users from different countries. As you can imagine, chosing inputs rather than outputs as indicators would lead to very different assessments of performance!

The management group reviewed the mission of the organization and decided that the use of the centre by people from different countries was a better indicator of the organization's success in meeting its objectives. However, not everyone readily agreed to this, as this indicator measured something beyond the centre's control.

EXERCISE 6. Developing indicators

Instructions: This exercise can help your team discuss and develop indicators. To get a sense of how different people view the same issue, it might be a good idea to work individually on developing indicators and then share your ideas.

Select one of the performance issues you identified in Exercise 5 (p. 20). Develop three to five key indicators you think should be monitored.

_____

_____

_____

Have you monitored these indicators in the past?

_____

_____

Does your organization have the ability to retrieve the information needed to monitor these indicators? If not, what would you have to put in place to collect the information – and is this possible?

_____

_____

_____

WHAT ARE THE BEST SOURCES OF DATA?

Essentially, data can be collected from two sources: documents and people. Document sources can be internal (financial statements, annual reports, human-resource policy, program-planning documents, strategic plans, promotion brochures, evaluation reports, etc.) or external (country policies, legislation, media, donor's reports, etc.). Here, the important point is to make sure that you review the documents that are appropriate for your strategic questions.

Data can also be obtained through people, either individually or in groups, either directly through conversation or indirectly through questionnaires. Who to meet is always a question. Ideally, you want to meet as many people as possible who can provide you with relevant information, but time constraints, political sensitivity, people's availability, and geographical location can limit the number of people you have access to. Deciding who will be your best sources of data is like identifying your key stakeholders.

When the time comes to make this decision, refer back to Exercise 3 (p. 9), in which you identified your major stakeholders. For an organizational assessment, you will definitely need information from senior management. You may also decide to collect information from staff or nonstaff (professional, support, board members, volunteers). Depending on your strategic questions, you may also want data from outside people, such as your beneficiaries, members, and donors.

In trying to match your sources of data with the issues, you may have to make some trade-offs. In seeking the best sources of data, you will also need to consider what is realistic, feasible, and acceptable.

WHAT METHODS WILL BE USED TO COLLECT DATA?

You can collect data in a variety of ways, such as through surveys, interviews, document reviews, and focus groups. To use these data-collection methods your team will have to develop the appropriate instrumentation.

OVERVIEW OF DATA-COLLECTION METHODS

Questionnaire survey
- This involves a printed or electronic list of questions
- This is distributed to a predetermined selection of individuals
- Individuals complete and return questionnaire

Face-to-face interview
- This involves personal interaction
- Interviewer asks questions, normally following a guide or protocol
- Interviewer records answers

Telephone interview
- This is like a face-to-face interview, but it is conducted over the telephone
- Interviewer records responses

Group technique (interview, facilitated workshop, focus group)
- This involves group discussion of predetermined issue or topic
- Group members share certain common characteristics
- Facilitator or moderator leads the group
- Assistant moderator usually records responses
- This can be conducted in person or through teleconferencing if available

Document review
- This involves identification of written or electronic documents (reports, journals, etc.) containing information on issues to be explored
- Researchers review documents and identify relevant information
- They keep track of the information retrieved from documents

WHICH DATA-COLLECTION METHOD WILL WE USE?

Use a surface-mail or faxed questionnaire survey when

- The target population is large (for example, greater than 200)
- You require a large amount of categorical data
- You want or require quantitative data and statistical analyses
- You want to examine the responses of designated subgroups, such as male and female
- The target population is geographically dispersed
- You want to clarify your team's objectives by involving team members in a questionnaire-development exercise
- You have access to people who can process and analyze this type of data accurately

Use an e-mail or web-page questionnaire when all of the above conditions are met and

- You have the appropriate software and knowledge of this method
- Your respondents have the technological capabilities to receive, read, and return the questionnaire
- Time is of the essence
- You want to provide the option of typing long answers to questions
- You want to reduce production and dissemination costs

Use face-to-face interviews when

- You need to incorporate the views of key people (key-informant interview)
- The target population is small (for example, less than 50)
- Your information needs call for depth rather than breadth
- You have reason to believe that people will not return a questionnaire

Use telephone interviews when

- The target population is geographically dispersed
- Telephone interviews are feasible

Use a teleconference interview when

- The target population is geographically dispersed
- Teleconferencing equipment is in place

Use group techniques when

- You need rich description to understand client needs
- You believe that group synergy is necessary to uncover underlying feelings
- You have access to a skilled facilitator and data recorder
- You want to learn what the stakeholders want through the power of group observation (one-way mirror or video)

Use document reviews when

- The relevant documents exist and are accessible
- You need a historical perspective on the issue
- You are not familiar with the organization's history
- You need hard data on selected elements of the organization

Before selecting a method and developing instruments, however, you will want to consider the following:

- The type of information you are seeking (Is it readily available? Is it very sensitive?);
- The resources available to collect data (Do you have the time, money, and people skilled in developing instruments?); and
- The values and attitudes both inside and outside your organization, concerning data-collection methods (What level of external credibility is necessary? What rigour of data will be needed to back up findings?).

YOU MIGHT BE IN FOR A SURPRISE

In one organization, the support and cleaning staff had never been invited to participate in any aspect of organizational life.

We experimented during the self-assessment process and chose to seek their opinion through focus groups, as some of the staff could neither read nor write. We trained a local person to conduct a focus group in the local language.

Because this was a completely new idea in this organization, we warned the facilitator that he should invite between 20 and 25 persons to get a turnout of 10–12 persons. We also told him that the focus group might not last the whole 90 minutes.

Well, all 25 people showed up, and the focus group lasted 2 hours!

"Never," said a janitor who attended the session, "had anyone asked me anything about this organization," even though he had been working in it since the beginning and probably had the biggest corporate memory of the group!

KNOW YOUR AUDIENCE!

In assisting with a self-assessment process in one institute, we had considerable time constraints. Because we were two facilitators and had only one afternoon to meet 16 professional staff members, we decided to conduct two focus groups.

What we didn't realize was that the culture of this centre was unconducive to group sharing, and the issues we were examining were perceived as very sensitive.

One staff member came to us at lunch and asked us each to conduct, in 2 hours, eight 15-minute individual interviews, as the professional staff would not open up in a group setting. Even these short individual interviews provided rich data for the assessment.

STRENGTHS AND WEAKNESSES OF THE MOST COMMON DATA-COLLECTION METHODS

STRENGTHS	WEAKNESSES
SURFACE-MAIL OR FAXED QUESTIONNAIRES	
■ Is highly efficient for routine data collection with a large number of respondents ■ Lends itself to quantitative analysis and the use of powerful descriptive and inferential statistics ■ Records individual comments and perspectives in the respondent's own words ■ Enables use of a large number of questions ■ Is cost-efficient and timely ■ In many parts of the world, people are familiar with this type of data collection	■ Requires extensive planning and pretesting of instrument ■ People might not respond, because of "questionnaire fatigue" – leading to nonresponse bias ■ Permits no great depth in responses ■ Response rate is typically low ■ Misunderstanding of the questions is possible – leading to response bias ■ Accurate wording requires a cultural and contextual understanding of respondents
ELECTRONIC QUESTIONNAIRES *	
■ Is quick to send, and erroneous addresses are caught within seconds ■ Is quick and easy for the respondent to complete and return ■ Is extremely cost-efficient if you have the technology ■ Software enables you to control the visual presentation of web-page questionnaires and eliminates the need for data entry (not with e-mail questionnaires) ■ Reminders, follow-up activities, and acknowledgments are quick and easy ■ If the person receiving the questionnaire is away, an associate who is reading the mail may inform you – so you are aware of why the questionnaire has not been answered	■ Assumes people have access to and can use a computer and e-mail or the Internet ■ You cannot control for the visual appearance of the e-mail questionnaires as received ■ Not everyone regularly checks his or her e-mail ■ E-mail questionnaires demand more from the respondent ■ Technology intimidates some people; they will not use it but may request that a hard copy be faxed or mailed ■ Because electronic questionnaires are new, you may have to duplicate your efforts and contact some people electronically; others, using hard copy ■ Requires a person with the knowledge and skills to develop electronic questionnaires
PRESENTATION	
■ Allows for discussion ■ Allows presenter to focus discussion	■ May be inefficient use of team time ■ May fail to focus on key issues ■ Gives limited time for in-depth questioning

* The strengths and weaknesses of "surface-mail or faxed questionnaire" (above) also apply to this method of data collection.

STRENGTHS AND WEAKNESSES OF THE MOST COMMON DATA-COLLECTION METHODS – *continued*

STRENGTHS	WEAKNESSES
FACE-TO-FACE INTERVIEW	
■ Shows value placed on individual client	■ Personal nature may lead respondents to say things just to please the interviewer
■ Allows for in-depth analysis and pursuit of details geared to each respondent	■ Requires careful planning of questions when multiple interviewers are used; also requires training
■ Few respondents refuse to be interviewed, leading to 100% response and good validity for the sample interviewed	■ Validity relies on skilled interviewers ■ Is logistically difficult to arrange for efficient interviews ■ Is time-consuming for all parties, expensive ■ Is often difficult to analyze in ways that give clear directions
TELEPHONE INTERVIEW	
■ Has many of the advantages of face-to-face interviews but at considerably lower cost ■ Telephones permit rapid coding of responses on paper or computer ■ Protocol and answers can be computer driven	■ Some respondents consider it intrusive ■ The interviewer often cannot maintain the respondent's attention for an extended period
GROUP TECHNIQUE	
■ Uses group synergy to maximize recall and highlight the diversity of perspectives ■ Provides rich qualitative perspectives ■ Group process can uncover underlying attitudes ■ Allows you to reach a large number of people in a short time	■ Requires extensive question and logistics planning ■ Depends on the team's having a skilled group facilitator ■ Does not easily lend itself to quantification ■ Participants sometimes feel that they cannot speak openly
DOCUMENT REVIEW	
■ Is economical ■ Provides a good source of general background ■ Is unobtrusive ■ May bring issues to the surface not noted by other means	■ Information may be inapplicable, disorganized, unavailable, or out of date ■ Could be biased because of "selective survival" of information ■ May require research efforts ■ May turn up unreliable statistics
OBSERVATION	
■ Provides eye-witness accounts ■ Allows comparison of words and deeds ■ Is sensitive when used by a trained observer ■ Occurs in a natural setting	■ May create artificial situations ■ May give inadequate sampling of observed events ■ Costs a lot in time and personnel ■ May reflect observer bias

EXERCISE 7. Selecting methodologies

Instructions: This exercise can help your self-assessment team select the most appropriate and efficient methods for data collection.

Working across the self-assessment matrix, your team has identified issues, developed key questions, and designed indicators. The next step will be to determine the best source of data for each indicator and the method to be used to collect the data.

Here's an example. To help them determine the effectiveness of their research institution, a self-assessment team developed the following question: "To what extent is the institution producing high-quality research?" One of the indicators they developed was the number of research papers published in refereed journals each year. Their matrix looked like the one below.

Indicator	Source of data	Methodology
Number of research publications	CVs of staff researchers	Content analysis of staff CVs

Working with the indicators you developed in Exercise 6 and the resources available to you, what sources of data and methods for data collection would you use?

Indicator	Source of data	Methodology

SEE APPENDICES 2 & 3

See tips for designing questionnaires, conducting interviews, etc., in Appendix 2. Also, see Sample 1 (staff questionnaire) and Sample 2 (donor questionnaire) in Appendix 3 (p. 113).

EXERCISE 8. Completing the self-assessment matrix

Instructions: Now that you have reviewed the whole matrix, step by step, you are ready to complete the entire self-assessment matrix for your organization.

Make a matrix for yourself like the one shown below. Complete the matrix, using the information you have already compiled by doing Exercises 5–7. It is easier to work across the sheet for each issue, developing questions, indicators, sources of data, and methods.

Major issue	Key question	Subquestion	Indicator	Source of data	Data-collection method
Effectiveness	How effective is the organization in moving toward fulfillment of its mission?	To what extent is the organization producing high-quality research (part of its mission)?	Number of papers published in journals	Staff CVs	Questionnaire or content analysis of CVs

HAVE YOU FORGOTTEN ANYTHING?

If you answer "no" to any of the questions below, review this chapter and complete the steps you need to get to "yes," before continuing with conducting a self-assessment in Chapter 3.

REVIEW QUESTIONS

YES NO

☐ ☐ Have you identified the major performance issues in your organization?

☐ ☐ Have you identified the probable causes of these performance problems (external-environment, motivational, capacity factors)?

☐ ☐ Have you identified a handful of indicators to help you to answer the questions you are exploring?

☐ ☐ Have you identified the most important sources of data?

☐ ☐ Are these sources accessible?

☐ ☐ Will your approach to data collection match your time constraints, the skills of your team, and the culture of your organization?

☐ ☐ Do you have the appropriate people to participate in data analysis?

C H A P T E R 3

Conducting a
Self-Assessment

. . . .

PLANNING FOR DATA COLLECTION

Collecting the data will be easier and yield better results if the process is carefully designed. Through careful planning, you will easily see flaws in the design and be able to allocate data-collection resources strategically. Beware, however, of overplanning, which can decrease your team's flexibility – a very important aspect of a successful self-assessment. Two useful tools for organizing data collection are the work breakdown and the person-day analysis. Actually, these tools are often used to organize an entire project (such as a self-assessment), not just the data-collection part, but this is a good place to introduce the concepts.

SEE TOOLS 5 & 6

See Tool 5 (work breakdown) and Tool 6 (person-day analysis) in Appendix 1 (pp. 90, 92).

The work breakdown should include one line for each group of activities or tasks (work package) small enough to be easily managed and for one person to be held accountable. For example, your self-assessment might include a questionnaire survey, and this will need to be designed, distributed, coded, and analyzed. These tasks may be broken into different work packages, or they may be grouped in other ways that make sense to you. The point is that each work package should have a definable output, a time frame, and a responsible person. Once you have done this for each data-collection task, you can allocate the tasks to team members as illustrated in the sample person-day analysis (Tool 6 in Appendix 1, p. 92).

Note that a common complaint from people engaged in such planning is that not enough time is available to do all the things the team would like to do. This need not be a major limitation if you think about the available resources and the best ways to use them. You can collect data in many different ways, and all these ways have strengths and weaknesses. Use the constraint as an opportunity to talk about what you really need and of alternative ways to understand the organization. It is better to be selective in data collection and do it well than to try to do everything and do it poorly.

In your planning for data collection, assign team members in ways that will take advantage of their strengths. Some people have experience in conducting interviews; others are familiar with questionnaires and surveys. Make sure that responsibilities are balanced and tasks are shared. Remember that the power of the assessment will be enhanced if participants feel that they have ownership of the processes leading to the results.

COLLECTING THE DATA

Your team will now be ready to begin formal data collection. Actually, because they work in the organization, team members will already have a great deal of information, impressions, and opinions. This type of knowledge is useful for shaping questions and instruments, but it is not systematic data.

The data-collection process should offer an opportunity to begin afresh – to wipe the slate clean of impressions, some of which may be incorrect. Indeed, one of the greatest problems with self-assessment processes is that people base their conclusions on previously held beliefs. One of the strengths of the process, in general, is that people are surprised by what they find when they study their organization seriously. Everyone in the organization will have more confidence in the process if it is clear that conclusions have been shaped by the data they provided.

The team must take several measures to ensure that self-assessment data are valid:

- Data-collection processes are strongest if it is clear from the beginning that everyone will have a chance to be heard on an equal basis;
- Data-collection instruments need to be well developed and agreed on so that every respondent can be asked to express views in a standardized way; and

- People leading interview or focus-group processes should not take things for granted; instead, they should explore or even challenge each response to ensure that they have not unintentionally filtered it themselves.

Be sure to capture the data in ways that other members of the team can learn from. Summarize interviews, analyze the information provided by focus groups, tabulate the contents of documents, and so forth – so that other team members can read and understand the material. Because the analysis should involve each team member, you must provide each other with the basic materials you will each need to participate.

Actual data collection is a typical human process that will no doubt occur differently from what you envisaged when you drew up your neatly categorized data-collection plan. It seldom takes place in an orderly, sequential manner. In many respects, the data-collection plan must be flexible to accommodate respondent's schedules and other obligations. Some people may be traveling when a questionnaire arrives. Others may be unable to attend a focus group at its scheduled time and place. Some individuals may not wish to be interviewed by a colleague, superior, or subordinate.

What do you do in such circumstances? Be flexible and have a team leader who can identify and solve such problems. Data collection is an organic process – it doesn't have the constraints of a physical or chemical experiment in which all conditions need to be strictly controlled. Try to include everyone on terms that they can deal with. Remember that the data set is rarely complete and never perfect.

ANALYZING YOUR DATA

Learning from your data can be a challenge. You may find that you collected a great deal of information but have difficulty making use of it. You need to make some decisions along the way, starting at the design stage of your assessment, to simplify the collection and use of data. Keep in mind that to understand what is going on, you don't need to collect every possible bit of information. You need to decide what is important, ensure variety in your data sources and types, and keep track of your original questions as a basis for sorting the data.

DATA NEEDS AND ACCESS TO SOURCES OF DATA

As the self-assessment process continues, think about your data needs and whether you have access to sources of data:

Access to a suitable spectrum of people, such as
- Administrators,
- Clients, stakeholders, and institutional representatives,
- Researchers, teachers, and support staff, and
- Government officials;

Access to key documents, such as
- Institution handbook, calendar, and prospectus,
- Mission statement,
- Annual report and financial reports, and
- Program descriptions;

Opportunities to observe relevant facilities and activities, such as
- Buildings and grounds,
- Laboratories,
- Program or project sites, and
- Teaching; and

Opportunities to observe the dynamics among people, such as
- Nature of meetings, who attends, and who presides,
- Processes for teaching and learning,
- Nature of dealings with the institution's clients, and
- How research is conducted and its dominant paradigm.

Data sources and triangulation

To understand the importance of the data you are collecting, you should be clear about the sources of the data. For example, if you are collecting data from only one group of people (such as senior management or line employees), then you need to take that into account in your analysis. The data will only reflect the views of that group, and you will have no way of knowing whether they reflect the general opinion of people in the organization. Ideally, you will collect data from more than one group, and you should also try to collect more than one type of data. If you only collect opinions but do not compare them with, for example, the organization's financial data or project results, then you may miss some key information. If you collect data from different sources, you can triangulate your data to reduce inconsistencies and confirm results from more than one source. You can build a much stronger interpretation with information that comes from several different sources.

Sorting the data

Finally, you should go back to your strategic questions and establish a frame-work to sort the data around the original issues. This is important because the actual questions you have asked may give you data to address more than one issue; it is also important because you can easily lose sight of your objective once you have a mass of information to deal with.

The data-collection process often yields some unexpected results. What do you do with data that fail to fit in with any of the questions or issues in your matrix? Your first consideration should probably be the importance of the information. If it seems clear to you that this is an important issue, or one sug-gested by several different data sources, you may want to add a question or subquestion to your matrix. If, on the other hand, the information is relatively unimportant – for example, it is the impression of only one person – you will likely just set it aside.

Three points to keep in mind in sorting the data are the following:

- *Look for patterns* – Look for information that agrees with or supports other information, look for trends, and look for information that contradicts other information. You may find patterns both within and across questions and categories.
- *Code your data* – If you code your data, you can review it later with original-source verification. Although you may not need to return to the data, going back through uncoded data is very time consuming. Code confidentially – to respect the confidentiality you offered your interviewees – but make the codes useful. For example, you might code managers as M1, M2, etc., and government stakeholders as G1, G2, etc., to help you keep track of sources.
- *Weight your data* – Weight your data to take into account how many intervie-wees gave you the same answer, whether the information is confirmed across different interest groups, and whether it is confirmed or denied by external sources. Assess the reliability of the data and the relative importance of the information to the question you are trying to answer. You will find that some data are more important than others, and the more important data should be given more weight.

Basis for judgment

Because you can interpret a set of data in many ways, it is important to take into account potential differences in interpretation early in the process. Three main decision-making methods are generally used to make judgments about the interpretation of data:

- *Comparison* – This involves a comparison of present with past organizational data, with accepted industry standards, or with practices found to work at other locations.
- *Expert opinion* – Experts are those who have good insight into the organization, are practitioners in organizational development, or have pertinent sectoral experience.
- *Criteria reference* – This data involves a comparison of organizational data with preestablished criteria (objectively verifiable indicators).

SEE APPENDIX 2

See Appendix 2 (p. 93) for tips on analyzing group, interview, and questionnaire data.

COMMUNICATING THE RESULTS

Communication will be important throughout and after the self-assessment process. How you handle this issue will depend on who needs to obtain self-diagnosis information and how they wish to receive it. Therefore, very early in the process you should decide with each of the various audiences how they will get information on the self-assessment, both during and after the process. The matrix below can help you keep track of this aspect of the process.

COMMUNICATING RESULTS DURING AND AFTER THE PROCESS			
Audience for the process	What the audience needs to know	How I will communicate about the process during the process	How I will communicate about the process after the process
[Example] Staff, Board of Directors, funder		[Example] Briefing at staff meetings, memos, progress reports, summary, verbal presentations	[Example] Final written report, verbal debriefing, videos, displays

Communicating during the process

Specific procedures should be designed to ensure that everyone involved in the data-collection process is kept informed and has an opportunity to be heard. These procedures might include

- Regularly scheduled subgroup meetings (survey team, interview team, etc.) to review progress, identify problems, and develop alternatives;
- Specific communication mechanisms during data collection (fax, e-mail, conference calls);
- Periodic meetings, involving the entire assessment team, to update everyone on progress;
- Negotiated time during formal meetings to communicate progress to others; and
- A final team-debriefing session.

Communicating after the process

After the self-assessment process, your team will likely undertake some of the following activities:

- Conducting information sessions on the results of the diagnosis;
- Distributing a memo on the results of the diagnosis; and
- Writing a report, if that was agreed on.

Information can be conveyed in ways that are traditional or creative, or both. The team should be prepared to go further than the diagnosis, but you must keep in mind the issues on which you can reasonably expect action.

Hints for conveying results

- *Know your audience* – Conveying the assessment results requires knowledge of the person or group listening to you.
- *Climate* – Creating a proper climate for conveying your results is a critical ingredient in communication. An atmosphere of trust is essential. Develop a session in which there are to be no winners or losers, one in which everyone benefits.
- *Purpose* – The team should set objectives for the session. What are the most important things to get across? Which are the less important ones?
- *Type of feedback* – Individuals may provide written information, or the group may be asked for oral comments.
- *Organization of the information session* – Give some thought to the beginning,

middle, and end of your information session. You might want to start with global comments, then add detailed findings, and end with a question-and-answer period.

- Be *creative* – You want to leave a good impression about the results. Think about alternative ways to tell the story, and don't be afraid to add an element of surprise if it will help people learn. Oral presentations, videos, and displays can often be more memorable and effective than written reports.

Writing a good report

If you have agreed to write a report on the self-assessment for a group or groups in your audience, ensure it is clear and that it meets the needs of its audience. Nobody likes to write or read extremely long or complicated reports. A good assessment report:

- Describes the purpose of the assessment and appends the terms of reference;
- Answers the questions posed in the terms of reference;
- Describes the methods used to collect and analyze the data;
- Indicates any limitations of the assessment or its methodology;
- Indicates the reliability and validity of the data used;
- Includes the major data, suitably analyzed, on which the conclusions are based;
- Describes any samples drawn and the number of targeted and available elements; and
- Contains an executive summary that outlines the purpose, methods, key questions, and findings of the self-assessment.

WHAT ISSUES MAY ARISE AT THIS STAGE?

It is difficult to predict how a self-assessment will go. In our experience in the past, each case seemed unique. However, some themes came up with more frequency than others, and we list these here so that you will know nothing is unusual about your own situation if you come across any of them:

- Denial of data or resistance by management or other members of the organization;
- Little match between questions asked and available resources and data;
- Difficulty analyzing appropriate key questions;
- Unclear answers to key questions;
- A failure to obtain enough data to answer the question;

REPORTING ON THE SELF-ASSESSMENT

Allow your institution to frame findings in a way that will be heard
We experimented with the self-assessment process in several countries in the same region. Although overall there were similarities in the culture of the region, the researchers had training in several different traditions.

In one research institution, the researchers had been trained in the Anglo-Saxon tradition; in another, in the French tradition.

Although no significant difference could be found in the depth of the analysis, major differences were found in the ways the researchers chose to report their findings. The ones with Anglo-Saxon training were more direct, even blunt, in their presentation of findings and recommendations. Those with a French training preferred to contextualize the process, the findings, and the recommendations.

Presenting the findings
In one organization, we suggested presenting findings in a very concise way; a brief statement of each finding, followed by a paragraph with supporting data.

The self-assessment team rejected this method for presenting the findings and suggested presenting them in a "softer" paragraph so that they would not "jump out" at the reader. As a rule, people gave feedback in a less direct manner in this region than in North America, and the report had to reflect that.

The message can be shared in many ways
In one organization, the self-assessment team indicated that it had to give a final report to various audiences and had to use different methods of communication for each:
- For one of their funders, the team wrote a substantive report;
- For internal staff, the team presented the main findings at a 1-hour staff meeting;
- For the Board of Directors, the team wrote a short version of the report, with an additional section entitled "Actions to be taken by the Board"; and
- As the 20th anniversary of the centre was approaching, the team included highlights of the report in the organization's corporate profile, which it used to invite potential donors to support the organization.

Keep us posted
At one research centre, the beginning of the self-assessment process was announced at one of the daily staff meetings. All staff members had an opportunity to ask questions about the purpose, the expected results, and the reasons for starting the process. From then on, every few weeks throughout the process, the staff received a brief progress report on the self-assessment. The executive director received private weekly briefings.

- Questionable validity or reliability of data;
- The need to ensure that questions are answered;
- Contradictory data;
- Sensitive data, difficult to report;
- Limited depth of information;
- Disagreement about the meaning of data and about exact findings;
- Difficulty assigning levels of effort for each stage of assessment: data collection, analysis, communication;
- A tendency to evaluate the performance of individuals, rather than that of the organization; and
- Evidence of wrongdoing.

DENYING THE DATA

In one organization, we encountered some difficulty with people's denial of data. In individual interviews, professional staff expressed some very controversial views on the management approach. They insisted that the research centre was becoming a consulting firm, responding to external demands instead of fulfilling its mission (which was to conduct research that the local government could use in its decision-making).

When we shared a summary of these data with the management group, they denied that staff gave these data to the self-assessment team. They indicated that the staff members we had interviewed (8 out of 111 of their professionals) were unaware of the facts. Although the management group said they would provide us with exact data by the following day, they did not do so.

Authors' note: There is not always an answer; self-assessment is a case-by-case effort.

HOW WILL THE RESULTS BE USED?

The self-assessment is not an end in itself but a process of diagnosis and reflection that should lead to action. Unfortunately, some organizations stop short of action. They stop once the diagnosis is complete and fail to act on the results. If you need to use the results of your self-assessment to improve your organization, make sure the results do not get shelved or ignored.

Why results get shelved

Some of the reasons why results get shelved are beyond your control, but others can be avoided through good planning and communication. Here are the four most common reasons:

- From the beginning, no one had ownership for the self-assessment process or its results.
- The diagnosis was not strategically conceived, it answered the wrong questions, and it addressed the wrong audience.
- The context of the organization changed so dramatically that the assessment findings were no longer relevant.
- Leaders were no longer interested in the results, they did not have sufficient resources or interest to act on the findings, or they did not agree with the findings.

WHAT HAPPENED NEXT?

One organization continued the self-assessment process with a 3-day strategic planning exercise, in which the self-assessment data were used to develop strategies. Another organization used its self-assessment report to develop a special session of the Board of Directors at its annual meeting. A third organization never fully completed the exercise, because of various changes inside the organization. Little follow-up was conducted, and the draft report may have been shelved.

C H A P T E R 4

Diagnosing the Performance of Your Organization

. . . .

Identifying the main issues helps to define the focus of the self-assessment process. The following sections will help you develop deeper, more detailed strategic questions. We have provided a brief section on each component of the performance model; these have been adapted and refined from our earlier work, *Institutional Assessment*. Use the following sections in any order to focus on areas you wish to explore.

A FRAMEWORK FOR ASSESSING ORGANIZATIONAL PERFORMANCE

The International Development Research Centre (IDRC) and Universalia Management Group have constructed a framework to help organizations assess themselves. Our approach can help you clarify important issues and guide the collection of data to help you make decisions to improve your organization's performance and capacity.

In brief, the framework encompasses four areas:

ORGANIZATIONAL PERFORMANCE

External environment
- Administrative and legal
- Sociocultural
- Technological
- Stakeholder
- Economic
- Political

Organizational performance
- Effectiveness
- Efficiency
- Relevance
- Financial viability

Organizational motivation
- History
- Mission
- Culture
- Incentives or rewards

Organizational capacity
- Strategic leadership
- Human resources
- Financial management
- Organizational processes
- Program management
- Infrastructure
- Interinstitutional linkages

Your organization's performance is made visible through the activities it conducts to achieve its mission. Outputs and their effects are the most observable aspects of an organization's performance.

Ideas about the concept of performance vary considerably. Each interest group or stakeholder may have an entirely different idea of what counts. For instance, administrators might define your organization's performance in terms of the amount of money brought into the organization through grants, whereas a donor might define performance in terms of your organization's beneficial impact on a target group.

In our experience, very few organizations have performance data readily available. However, it is usually not difficult to generate this information from existing data or to develop mechanisms for gathering performance data.

Data gathering tends to be mechanical and technical. It is far more difficult to obtain consensus on the merits of particular performance data and indicators. It is even more difficult to arrive at value judgments regarding acceptable levels of quantity and quality for each performance indicator. The real questions are these: How does your organization define good performance? Does good performance help your organization attain its mission? The second of these questions is particularly important for organizations that have very diverse stakeholders.

When you are diagnosing your organization and its performance, the number and choice of indicators are critical. "Wise" organizations try to identify 10–15 key performance indicators that they can regularly monitor to assess their own performance. It is also wise to have a set of other variables to monitor as a barometer to help understand performance. These other variables may include employee morale, timeliness of financial information, economic indicators, absenteeism, and number of new funders.

YOU MAY ALREADY HAVE INDICATORS

Although we have often worked with organizations that never went through the process of thinking about their indicators, we have found that every organization has a unique set of organizationally appropriate indicators. Your organization needs to create its own indicator-monitoring list. Not all the indicators you develop will have the same importance, and you may also find that the appropriate indicators change as your organizational-performance issues do or as the organization evolves.

Effectiveness

The effectiveness of your organization is the degree to which it moves toward the attainment of its mission and realizes its goals. Effectiveness, however, is not a simple concept. The basic difficulty in analyzing effectiveness lies in the fact that many organizations make multiple statements about their missions and goals. Sometimes these statements are in the organization's charter; other times, in their strategic documents. Regardless of where you find these statements, you need a clearly defined guide to the raison d'être of the organization.

A BALANCING ACT

One research institution was caught in a dilemma that many funded institutions can relate to. External donors offered to fund it to carry out environmental-impact projects. Although fascinating and lucrative, these projects would lie outside the mission of the institute, which was primarily to promote economic and social-science research. In addition, the research institute would have to hire an expert in environmental issues to carry out the projects. If the institute accepted this funding, the results of the research would not be fully used by the national government, but the institute would gain revenues from external donors.

The dilemma for this organization was to understand the trade-off between ensuring its own financial sustainability and working toward its mission.

EFFECTIVENESS ISSUES

How effective is your organization in working toward its mission?

- The charter, mission statement, and other documents provide the raison d'être for the organization.
- The mission is known and agreed to by staff.
- The mission is operationalized through program goals, objectives, and activities.
- Quantitative and qualitative indicators are used to capture the essence of the mission.
- A system is in place to assess effectiveness.
- The organization monitors organizational effectiveness.
- The organization uses feedback to improve itself.

SOME INDICATORS OF EFFECTIVENESS

- Number of clients served
- Quality of services or products
- Changes with respect to equality
- Environmental changes
- Quality-of-life changes
- Service access and usage
- Knowledge generation and use
- Collaborative arrangements
- Demand for policy or technical advice from stakeholders
- Replication of the organization's programs by stakeholders
- Growth indicators in terms of coverage of programs, services, clients, and funding

Efficiency

An organization must be able not only to provide exceptional services but also to provide them within an appropriate cost structure. Performance is increasingly judged by the efficiency of the organization (for example, the cost per service, the number of outputs per employee, the number of outputs per person per year, the average value of grants per person). Whatever the overall size of the unit, performing organizations are viewed as those that provide good value for the money in both quantitative and qualitative terms.

EFFICIENCY ISSUES

How efficient is your organization in the use of its human, financial, and physical resources?

- Staff members are used by the organization to the best of their abilities.
- Maximal use is made of physical facilities (buildings, equipment, etc.).
- Optimal use is made of financial resources.
- The administrative system provides good value for cost.
- High-quality administrative systems are in place (financial, human resources, program, strategy, etc.) to support the efficiency of the organization.
- Benchmark comparisons are made of the progress achieved in the organization.

- Cost per program
- Cost per client served
- Cost–benefit of programs
- Output per staff
- Employee absenteeism and turnover rates
- Program-completion rates
- Overhead – total program cost
- Frequency of system breakdowns
- Timeliness of service delivery

Relevance

Organizations in any society take time to evolve and develop, but they must develop in ways that consolidate their strengths. Organizations face internal and external crises, and no organization is protected from becoming out of date, irrelevant, or subject to closure. To survive, your organization must adapt to changing contexts and capacities and keep its mission, goals, programs, and activities agreeable to its key stakeholders and constituents.

RELEVANCE ISSUES

Has your organization remained relevant?

- Regular program revisions reflect changing environment and capacities.
- The mission is undergoing review.
- Stakeholder-needs assessments are conducted regularly.
- The organization regularly reviews the environment to adapt its strategy.
- The organization monitors its reputation.
- The organization creates or adapts to new technologies.
- Innovation is encouraged.
- The organization regularly undertakes role analyses.

SOME INDICATORS OF RELEVANCE

- Stakeholder satisfaction (clients, donors, etc.)
- Number of new programs and services
- Changes in partner attitudes
- Changes in role
- Changes in funders (quality and quantity)
- Changes in reputation among peer organizations
- Changes in reputation among key stakeholders
- Stakeholders' acceptance of programs and services
- Support earmarked for professional development
- Number of old and new financial contributors (risk of discontinuance, leverage of funding)
- Changes in organizational innovation and adaptiveness (changes appropriate to needs, methods)
- Changes in services and programs related to changing client systems

ARE WE ADEQUATELY BALANCING STAKEHOLDERS DEMANDS?

A social-service agency had to balance its ways of being relevant to its beneficiaries and funders:

- *Beneficiaries* – Because of increasing demands from the community to provide more home care for the elderly, the agency was tempted to put more of its resources into this type of service.
- *Funders* – One of its funders wanted the agency to increase its promotion and advocacy for voluntary work in and beyond the immediate community.

The Board of Directors and management were thus faced with two not necessarily convergent sets of demands from two important stakeholders.

Financial viability

To survive, your organization's inflow of financial resources must be greater than the outflow. Our experience has shown that the conditions needed to make an organization financially viable include multiple sources of funding, positive cash flow, and financial surplus.

FINANCIAL-VIABILITY ISSUES

Is your organization financially sustainable?

- Existing funding sources offer sustained support.
- The organization consistently obtains new funding sources.
- The organization consistently has more revenue than expenses.
- Assets are greater than liabilities.
- The organization keeps a reasonable surplus of money to use during difficult times.
- The organization monitors finances on a regular basis.
- Capital assets and depreciation are monitored.
- The organization does not depend on a single source of funding.

SOME INDICATORS OF FINANCIAL VIABILITY

- Changes to net operating capital over 3 years
- Ratio of largest funder to overall revenues
- Ratio of cash to deferred revenues
- Ratio of current assets to current liabilities
- Ratio of total assets to total liabilities
- Growth in terms of number of funders, amount of resources mobilized, assets, capital, and revenues
- Levels of diversification of funding sources
- Partners hired to provide services on a regular basis

EXERCISE 9. Analyzing organizational performance

Instructions: This is a good time to go back and review the performance issues you identified in Exercise 5 (Chapter 2, p. 20). Afterward, fill in the table below to show

- The problematic aspects of your organization's performance (effectiveness, efficiency, relevance, financial viability);
- Some of the signs (indicative issues) that tell you these are problems; and
- Some questions you could ask to allow you to assess the extent of each problem.

Main performance issue	Signs of the problem	Questions to ask to help assess the extent of the problem
Effectiveness [Example] Producing excellent research	[Example] Only 10% of the people on staff have had a refereed article published in the past 3 years	[Example] How many staff have submitted articles for publication? Does the organization encourage or reward publication? Does the organization plan or allow time for staff members to work on articles they wish to publish?
Efficiency		
Relevance		
Financial viability		

EXTERNAL ENVIRONMENT

Your organization does not exist in a vacuum. It is located in a country and region to which it is inextricably linked. It operates within a legal and cultural context. These and other external-environment variables influence how your organization operates and what it produces. Such variables can shape the ways your organization defines itself and the ways it defines good performance. You undertake an analysis of the external environment to understand the external forces that help to shape your organization.

The key dimensions of the external environment that influence your organization are the administrative, legal, political, sociocultural, economic, technological, and stakeholder contexts. Each of these components of the external environment is discussed individually in this section.

We have not provided types of indicators for the external environment because these are specific to each organization and its context.

WHY BOTHER?

Some organizations' staff members were a bit perplexed by our suggesting they assess the external environment: "There is very little we can do to change the external environment, so what is the purpose of assessing these external factors?" This statement is only partially true.

Generally, your organization will have a limited ability to change its environment, but the better you understand it, the better you can adapt to it and develop appropriate strategies. Most organizations are influenced by, and can influence, their environment.

Administrative and legal environment

Your initial task in mapping out the external environment will be to take a closer look at the current situation in terms of the organizations involved and their roles, influence, and effectiveness. You will need to understand the wider influences, such as laws and policies, that affect your organization.

ADMINISTRATIVE- AND LEGAL-ENVIRONMENT ISSUES

How is your organization affected by the administrative and legal environment?

Administrative

To what extent

- Is your organization influenced by the rules of other organizations, institutions, and groups to which it relates or might be expected to relate?
- Is your organization influenced by expectations of consumers, policymakers, suppliers, competitors, and other organizations in its external environment?
- Are your organization's objectives and activities influenced by governments, donors, and other organizations?
- Is your organization influenced by important sector rules and regulations?
- Do administrative norms and values in your country support or hinder the work that the organization intends to carry out?

Legal

To what extent

- Do the laws of the country support the role played by your organization?
- Does the legal framework support the organization's autonomy?
- Is the legal framework clear?
- Is the legal framework consistent with current practice?
- Is the legal regulatory context conducive to your organization's work?
- Does your organization monitor changes in the legal context which could affect the position of the organization?

Political environment

The quality of government in your external environment is a key determinant of your organization's performance and its prospects for change. The legitimacy, accountability, and transparency of this government will be centrally important to your organization.

POLITICAL-ENVIRONMENT ISSUES

How is your organization affected by the political environment?

To what extent

- Do the political and ideological trends of the government support the kind of work the organization does?
- Does the government system facilitate collaborative arrangements?
- Does the organization play a role in national or sector development?
- Does the organization have access to government funding?
- Does the organization have access to international funding?
- Does the organization have access to the government's knowledge and publications?
- Do government policies and programs support the organization?

Sociocultural environment

Every organization is to some degree affected by its sociocultural environment. It is important to develop an understanding of the wider public service and society in which your organization operates. This may include a better understanding of the inherent values of cultural and ethnic groups present in external communities.

SOCIOCULTURAL-ENVIRONMENT ISSUES

How is your organization affected by the sociocultural environment?

To what extent
- Is equity in the workplace a social value?
- Does the organization account for the effect of culture on program complexity?
- Do values found in the sociocultural environment support the work of the organization?
- Does the organization have access to a pool of capable human resources to recruit staff?
- Does the organization analyze and link demographic trends to its work?

Economic environment

The economic environment comprises the forces and trends affecting the availability and worth of an organization's resources. Is government spending more or less? If government is spending more, do its expenditures pertain to your organization? Is inflation under control or is it running rampant? Inflation decreases available resources. Similarly, it is important for you to know whether donors or other foreign investors are making more or fewer resources available. Government policy will affect all these conditions in the economic environment.

ECONOMIC-ENVIRONMENT ISSUES

How is your organization affected by the economic environment?

To what extent
- Does the government's economic policy support the organization's ability to acquire technologies and financial resources?
- Is money available to do the organization's work?
- Is the organization supported by donors?

Technological environment

Understanding the types and levels of technology in a society gives insight into the nature of the organizations that operate in that society. For instance, if your organization generally deals with Western models and concepts, you will depend on different technologies than organizations carrying out indigenous research. It is important to understand the level of relevant technology in the organization's context and to consider the processes for introducing new technology.

TECHNOLOGICAL-ENVIRONMENT ISSUES

Do systems in the wider environment support the technology needed for your organization's work?

To what extent
- Is adequate physical infrastructure (power, telecommunication, transport) in place to support the organization's work?
- Is the technology needed for your organization's work supported by the overall level of national-technology development?
- Does the government system facilitate the organization's process for acquiring needed technology?
- Is the level of human-resource development in your organization adequate to support new technology?

Stakeholder environment

Stakeholders commonly include individuals, groups, or organizations with an interest or a stake in your organization. They typically include the Board of Directors, beneficiaries, suppliers, governments, staff members, unions, competitors, local communities, and the general public. Each of these groups can justifiably expect (or in some cases, require) your organization to responsibly satisfy its expectations.

Therefore, stakeholder analysis is an important source of information for a self-assessment. It is important to identify your stakeholders and understand their roles and their expectations vis-à-vis your organization. It is also important to assess their perceptions of the issues and challenges facing your organization, the resources (political, legal, human, and financial) they may contribute to help your organization address those challenges, their own mandates with respect to your organization, their possible reactions to some of your organization's strategies, and the existing or potential conflicts between stakeholders.

STAKEHOLDER-ENVIRONMENT ISSUES

Does the stakeholder environment support your organization?

To what extent
- Is the community involved in the organization?
- Are partners involved in the organization?
- Do governments value the organization's products and services?
- Do governments request or use the organization's products and services?
- Do similar organizations compete or cooperate with your organization?
- Do donors influence the organization?
- Do funders support the organization?

SEE EXERCISE 3, TOOL 2 & EXERCISE A2

See Exercise 3 (mapping the stakeholders) in Chapter 1 (p. 9), Tool 2 (stakeholder assessment) in Appendix 1 (p. 86), and Exercise A2 (our external context) in Appendix 4 (p. 124).

EXERCISE 10. Understanding the organization's external environment

Instructions: This exercise can help the self-assessment team understand how the organization relates to its environment. One interesting way to do this exercise is to have a brainstorming session.

How would you characterize the external environment of your organization in relation to the performance issues you have identified? Is it hostile to or supportive of your performance?

_____

_____

_____

What specific aspects of the external environment do you think you should monitor?

Administrative and legal _____

Political _____

Sociocultural _____

Technological _____

Economic _____

Stakeholder _____

ORGANIZATIONAL MOTIVATION

External environment
- Administrative and legal
- Sociocultural
  - Technological
    - Stakeholder
      - Economic
      - Political

Organizational performance
- Effectiveness
- Efficiency
- Relevance
- Financial viability

Organizational motivation
- History
- Mission
- Culture
- Incentives or rewards

Organizational capacity
- Strategic leadership
- Human resources
- Financial management
- Organizational processes
- Program management
- Infrastructure
- Interinstitutional linkages

Organizations, like people, have different rhythms and personalities. Each has a different purpose, or mission. Some are highly motivated by the opportunity "to do good," whereas others are driven to perform by other forces, including the personal ambitions of key players. Each organization also has a unique working ambiance, or climate – a combination of purpose, history, and personality. The organizational concepts that drive your organization include its history, its mission, its internal culture, its incentives or rewards, and the widespread values and beliefs about the role your organization plays in society. We consider the first four of these – history, mission, culture, and incentives or rewards – as being the elements of organizational motivation.

Assessing the motivation of your organization can be a very sensitive task, as you are in fact digging into what the organization is. In our experiences with different organizations, we found that strategies to address changes in this area took a long time to implement. The older the organization, the more past history it carried and the more carefully it needed to approach changes in this area. Often, factors related to organizational motivation cause a change to fail.

History

Your organization's history is charted in its important milestones – the story of its beginnings, rate of growth, awards of achievement, and notable changes in structure or leadership. Although the organization's evolution or history is often expressed through formal documents – such as the charter, stated goals, objectives, and plans (strategic or otherwise) – it is also told in unwritten stories that can be highly motivating.

HISTORY ISSUES

What are the memorable events in your organization's history?

- The milestones
- The successes
- The crises

Mission: stated and perceived

Your organization's mission is its raison d'être. It answers certain questions: Why does this organization exist? Whom does it serve? By what means does it serve them? We often find, however, that these questions have two types of answer: the organization's written mission statement (stated) and the mission that we hear about from members of the organization (perceived).

The mission statement is the written expression of the basic goals, characteristics, values, and philosophy that shape your organization and give it purpose. This statement is an attempt to distinguish the organization from others by clearly defining its scope of activities; its products, services, and market; and the significant technologies and approaches it uses to meet its goals. The strength of your organization's mission is the degree to which the stated mission and the perceived mission are the same.

MISSION ISSUES

To what extent does the organization have a clear mission that drives members' behaviour?

- A clear mission drives the behaviour of the organization's members.
- The organization's mission is related to its goals.
- The organization's members have accepted its mission and feel they can ascribe to it.
- The mission is updated and linked to a set of goals.
- The key values and beliefs driving members' behaviour are linked to the mission.
- New staff embrace the mission.

Culture

The culture of your organization is the sum of the values, beliefs, customs, traditions, and meanings related to mission fulfilment. These have developed over the history of the organization, and they make it unique, govern its character, and drive the organization.

The characteristics that distinguish your organization are part of its culture. The culture incorporates all of your organization's symbols, myths, visions, pride, and the accomplishments of its past and present heroes. Stories about past successes and failures may illustrate values important to your organization (such as team work, gender equity, participation, transparency). These stories form a living history that guides the managers.

 SEE TOOL 4 — Culture Audit

See Tool 4 (culture audit) in Appendix 1 (p. 89).

CULTURE ISSUES

What aspects of your organization's culture help it to fulfil its mission?

- Documents outline the organization's values.
- The people in the organization identify with the organization's values.
- People have good morale in the organization.
- People have a high level of commitment to performance in the organization.
- People in the organization have a positive attitude toward change.
- Functioning systems are in place to reinforce the organization's values, such as those for promotions, incentives, and training.
- People in the organization exhibit good will toward each other.

THE "REAL" ISSUE

In one organization, poor performance was attributed to the lack of training and appropriate materials and technology. Although these factors affected the organization's performance, the main issue turned out to be conflicting cultures inside the research centre:

- Some of the staff members had their own incentive systems and rewards, as they were paid by the university with which the centre was associated.
- Other staff members depended solely on the organization's ability to generate research projects, and these members were more entrepreneurial.

Incentives

Organizational incentives are the ways your organization's system of rewards and punishments either encourages or discourages certain behaviours. Incentives are important to individual careers and to the overall success of the organization. It is important to assess how employees at all levels of the organization view the effectiveness of the incentive system.

INCENTIVE ISSUES

Does the incentive system in your organization encourage or discourage members' performance?

- People feel they are rewarded for their work.
- People are adequately compensated.
- Nonmonetary rewards support good behaviour.
- The incentive system is adequately managed.
- The incentive system is under ongoing review.
- People are equitably treated in the organization.
- The organization is consistent between what it rewards people for and what it says it will reward people for.

SEE TOOL 4 & APPENDIX 3

See Tool 4 (culture audit) in Appendix 1 (p. 89) and Sample 1 (staff questionnaire) in Appendix 3 (p. 113).

EXERCISE 11. Determining organizational motivation

Instructions: This exercise can help you identify how your organization's history and past and present culture affect its performance and are related to its environment.

To make this more specific to your context and to help your team generate more useful data, we suggest you consider Tool 4 (culture audit) in Appendix 1 (p. 89) and Sample 1 (staff questionnaire) in Appendix 3 (p. 113). You could adapt and distribute these instruments and use the data to respond to the question below.

Based on your culture audit and staff survey, how do you think the mission, history, culture, and values of your organization affect its performance?

_____

_____

_____

_____

ORGANIZATIONAL CAPACITY

In our framework, the capacity of an organization is considered in terms of seven main, interrelated areas that we believe are the foundation of the organization's performance: strategic leadership, human resources, financial management, infrastructure, program management, process management, and interinstitutional linkages. Each of these areas contains various components, which range in importance among organizations.

In our experience, organizations often find capacity issues easier to identify and to address. This may be because it is easier to do something about them, whereas it may be impossible to change the external environment and difficult to change organizational motivation.

Similarly, donors may focus more on capacity-building because (1) organizations often request this type of support; (2) tangible changes can be seen in a relatively short time; and (3) an external body can make a contribution in this area (interventions to change the motivation or external environment may be unfeasible or inappropriate).

SEVEN AREAS OF ORGANIZATIONAL CAPACITY AND THEIR VARIOUS COMPONENTS

AREA	COMPONENTS
Strategic leadership	Leadership, strategic planning, governance, structure, and niche management
Human resources	Planning, staffing, developing, appraising and rewarding, and maintaining effective human-resource relations
Financial management	Financial planning, financial accountability, and financial statements and systems
Infrastructure	Facilities management and technology management
Program management	Planning, implementing, and monitoring programs and projects
Process management	Problem-solving, decision-making, communications, and monitoring and evaluation
Interinstitutional linkages	Planning, implementing, and monitoring networks and partnerships

Strategic leadership

Today, organizations need to be able to change quickly. They require leadership to link their internal and external realities so as to improve their own performance. We have used the term *strategic leadership* to convey these ideas.

In today's context, leadership is no longer seen in terms of the great-man theory; it requires many of the organization's members to take on leadership functions. Your leaders must have the ability to create and re-create long-term strategic plans and develop governance systems to support your organization's survival and development, structures to provide the balance between control and flexibility, and a niche for your organization to ensure it has unique or value-added roles in the economy. Our experience has shown that strategic leadership is an exceedingly complex undertaking.

To us, strategic leadership includes leadership, strategic planning, governance, organizational structure, and niche management. Each of these components is discussed individually in this section.

Leadership

Both formal and informal leadership can be found in many places inside your organization. Formal leadership is exercised by those appointed or elected to positions of authority. Formal leaders set the direction, ensure that tasks are done, and support resource development. Informal leadership, on the other hand, is exerted by persons who become influential because they possess special skills or resources valued or needed by others.

LEADERSHIP ISSUES

To what extent does strategic leadership affect your organization's performance?

- People have goals.
- The responsibilities for leadership and decision-making are known and distributed appropriately.
- The leaders in the organization are concerned to get significant tasks done well.
- The leaders in the organization are respected.
- Staff members are willing to take on leadership.
- People are willing to express new ideas to those in positions of power.
- The organization is appropriately linked externally, and its place is seen as important by peer organizations.
- Leadership is effective in acquiring and protecting resources.
- Leadership practices participatory management, and the Board of Directors and management work well together.
- Leadership is flexible, and it welcomes change.

Strategic planning

Strategic planning comprises the ways your organization thinks ahead and responds to its environment to achieve its goals. Strategic planning involves the development and implementation of activities that will lead to the long-term success of the organization. The strategic plan is a written document that sets out the specific values, mission, goals, priorities, and tactics that your organization will use to ensure good performance. It identifies gaps in the organization's performance and suggests ways to close these gaps.

With good strategic planning, your organization can anticipate and capitalize on opportunities in the external environment that might yield needed resources. It also means being able to predict threats to your resources so that you can intervene (typically, politically) to safeguard the organization's performance and survival.

STRATEGIC-PLANNING ISSUES

To what extent does strategic planning affect your organization's ability to achieve its goals?

- The organization has a strategic plan.
- The strategy is known to the Board of Directors, senior managers, researchers, and other staff.
- People in the organization generally accept and support the strategy.
- The strategy has helped clarify priorities, thus giving the organization a way to assess its performance.
- The strategy is used to help make decisions.
- The strategy improves performance.
- The strategy supports equity.
- The strategy helps the organization use resources optimally.
- The organization has a process for understanding its clients and users, for clarifying and revising its mission and beliefs, and for working to achieve its goals.
- The organization has a process for scanning the environment to consider potential threats and opportunities.
- The organizational strategy helps the organization to identify its opportunities and constraints in terms of financial resources and infrastructure.
- A process for monitoring the application of the strategy is in place.
- A similar process for understanding client and stakeholder requirements and changes is in place.
- The organization has a process for ongoing review and updating of its strategy to reflect internal and external realities.

Governance

The Board of Directors and charter of your organization provide its legal and policy framework and direction. A good Board of Directors has its finger on the pulse of both the internal and the external environments. The board assesses whether your organization's initiatives are supportable and meet development goals, nationally or regionally; whether your organization is responding appropriately to important forces and trends in its field and within the wider environment; and whether your organization is meeting the needs of those it serves.

GOVERNANCE ISSUES

To what extent does your organization's governance affect its performance?

- The governing structure both clarifies and supports the organization's direction.
- A charter provides an adequate framework for carrying out the mission of the organization and for dealing with external challenges to the organization.
- The governing body scans the external and internal environments to understand forces affecting the organization.
- The governing body responds appropriately to important environmental trends and influences, whether social, political, or economic. For instance, both quality and equality issues are reflected in the minutes and discussion. The governing body supports the principle of equity.
- The governing body operates effectively and efficiently.

Organizational structure

The structure of your organization is the system of working relationships that divides and coordinates the tasks of people and groups working with a common purpose. Most people imagine an organization's structure in terms of the familiar organigram (organization chart). However, structure is far more: it involves the division of labour (including roles, responsibility, and authority), as well the coordination of labour into units and inter- and intra-unit groupings. When you assess the structure of your organization, you will want to see if it facilitates or hinders the achievement of the mission and goals.

ORGANIZATIONAL-STRUCTURE ISSUES

Does your organizational structure facilitate or hinder your organization in achieving its mission or goals?

- The organization's structures support its mission and its goals.
- The roles within the organization are clearly defined but flexibly enough to adapt to changing needs.
- Departmental lines or divisions between groups are crossed easily, particularly when collaboration means an improved product, program, or service.
- Structural authority is used to further equity.
- Staff members have linkages with, and access to, other units in the organization important to their work.
- Coordinating mechanisms are in place to facilitate access to other units within the organization.
- Staff members can easily create important coordinating units.
- The organization encourages efficient ways to coordinate staff and units.
- The organization offers clear lines of accountability (individual, group, and organizational accountability).
- People have the authority to set an agenda to support accountability.
- The organization has efficiently functioning work groups.
- Decision-making is sufficiently decentralized to promote productivity and good morale.
- The structure relating to responsibility for performance makes organizational sense and facilitates the work.

Niche management

Niche management forces managers to look beyond internal matters to consider the wider environment and the broader issues of the time. It means carving out a particular area in the marketplace to match your organization's particular expertise. Your organization's niche helps to clarify its relations to similar local, regional, national, and international organizations. Your organization's niche helps determine the levels of funding and types of funders that can help build its capacity.

Does your organization undertake niche management to help it to achieve its mission and goals?

- The organization's constituents (stakeholders) understand its role or area of specialization.
- The role of the organization is clearly defined in its mission.
- The areas of specialization are clear.
- Stakeholders support the areas of specialization.
- The organization undertakes research and development that strengthens its unique role.

Human resources

The human resources of your organization include all staff (professional, managerial, technical, and support) engaged in any of your organization's activities. Your organization's human resources are perhaps its most valuable asset. This is particularly true if the people required to do the core work of your organization are highly trained individuals.

The human-resource-management function of your organization is responsible for ensuring that people's needs are met. This is not merely an altruistic function – staff members who are reasonably comfortable with working conditions and stimulated by the environment are highly likely to be productive. Human-resource management is responsible for planning; staffing; human-resource development; assessments and rewards; and maintaining effective human-resource relations. Each of these components of human-resource management will be reviewed individually in this section.

Planning

Human-resource planning is the first step in effective human-resource management. It involves forecasting the human-resource needs of your organization and planning the steps the organization must take to meet those needs. Human-resource planning should be closely linked to your organization's strategic objectives and mission. Even in regions with a plentiful, well-educated workforce, human-resource planning is a challenge because the needs of the organization are constantly changing and sometimes do not converge. The challenge is even greater if the recruitment pool is limited or if the people in charge of human-resource management have not been trained to forecast the organization's needs.

PLANNING ISSUES

To what extent does your organization's ability to plan for its human-resource needs affect its performance?

- The right people are in the right jobs in the organization.
- The organization can forecast current and future demands for human resources.
- The organization knows how and where to find the people with the skills needed to fill its needs.
- The organization can link its mission and goals to its human-resource planning.
- The organization has developed a personnel-policy manual.

CHANGING TIMES, CHANGING NEEDS

In changing times, it is not always easy to identify what kinds of people your organization will need. In one nonprofit organization, the mission and goals had been quite stable over the last decade. The organization paid little attention to the analysis of its human-resource demands. It continued to recruit people for the Board of Directors with the same profile as those who first made the organization a success: individuals with great dedication to the mission who were involved in the delivery of services and very interested in daily contact with direct beneficiaries.

Over the most recent 2 years, however, the organization had to privatize. It needed new staff members with a greater interest and skill in management, fundraising, and organizational issues. Although this organization was able to address the forecasting issue, it recognized that the search for a new staff profile was a challenge.

Staffing

Staffing for your organization means searching for, selecting, and orienting individuals with the appropriate range of knowledge, skills, behaviour, and values to meet your organization's needs.

STAFFING ISSUES

To what extent does your organization have adequate staffing procedures to ensure its performance?

- The organization has a staffing system.
- The organization has appropriate job descriptions or equivalents to determine the positions it is staffing for.
- The organization has an appropriate system for selecting candidates (for example, reviewing CVs, conducting interviews, checking references).
- Individuals in charge of selection are appropriately trained to carry out this function (interviewing and listening skills, politeness, good judgment).
- Recruitment and selection materials (advertisements, postings, interview questions) are neutral, free of discriminating elements (gender, religious, etc.).
- Someone who is familiar with the day-to-day functioning of the organization is available to orient new staff members.

Development

Developing human resources in your organization means improving employees' performance by increasing or improving their skills, knowledge, and attitudes. This allows your organization to remove or prevent performance deficiencies, makes your employees more flexible and adaptable, and can also increase their commitment to your organization. The development of human resources can take several forms, such as training for a job, training for a role inside the organization, and training for a career.

DEVELOPMENT ISSUES

To what extent does your organization have appropriate human-resource development systems and approaches to ensure its performance?

- The organization has a policy for training and development, as well as a budget for training.
- The organization encourages staff members to continue to learn and develop (by providing incentives for learning, by paying training costs, etc.).
- Someone in the organization can identify training needs.
- The organization supports application and transfer of new learning on the job.
- Training is demand driven (responds to needs in the organization), as opposed to supply driven (responding to whatever is being offered – on the market or by a donor).
- The organization can and does assess training and its effects on the organization's performance.
- The organization has plans for mentoring younger staff members to help them advance in their careers.
- The organization has a way of dealing with succession.
- People see career opportunities in the organization.

Assessments and rewards

The systems and approaches your organization uses to collect information and provide feedback on individuals or teams is an important aspect of your organization's human-resource management. This means assessing the contributions of each staff member and then distributing rewards (direct, indirect, monetary, and nonmonetary) according to the regulations of your region and to your organization's ability to pay. The assessment and reward system should aim at allowing your organization to retain good employees, motivate staff, administer pay, facilitate the organization's strategic objectives, and control labour costs.

ASSESSMENT AND REWARD ISSUES

To what extent does your organization have an appropriate system for assessment and reward that is fair and motivating?

- The organization has a compensation policy that complies with the rules and regulations of the country.
- Staff members see an adequate correlation between compensation and performance.
- Staff members are generally satisfied with their compensation.
- Compensation packages are externally competitive for the sector.
- The organization maintains internal equity of salaries and benefits (that is, equal compensation for work of equal value).
- Compensation differentials are appropriate to motivate staff.
- The organization motivates staff with both monetary and nonmonetary rewards.

Maintaining effective human-resource relations

The maintenance of effective human-resource relations applies to all the programs and systems your organization has put in place to ensure that employees are protected and dealt with in accordance with the appropriate legislation. It involves all the activities your organization has implemented to address health and safety issues, human-rights issues, and the quality of working life. In unionized settings, it involves collective bargaining. In essence, it represents the organization's culture, management style, and concrete measures taken to ensure that employees experience feelings of ownership, self-control, responsibility, and self-respect. Exactly what your organization does to produce these outcomes will vary according to the nature of the organization, its leadership style, and its cultural setting.

To what extent does your organization have effective human-resource relations?

- People in the organization feel protected from exploitation (through a collective agreement or through an appropriate set of personnel policies).
- Measures and procedures are established in the organization for dealing with people in emotional or physical distress.
- The organization seeks ways to increase the loyalty and the commitment of the staff.
- Morale in the organization is generally good.
- The organization has measures in place for dealing with harassment in the workplace.
- The organization has, if appropriate, a health and safety policy.
- Work-related accidents are rare.

Financial management

Your organization's ability to manage its financial resources is critical. Good management of budgeting, financial record-keeping, and financial reporting is essential to the overall functioning of your organization. Good financial management ensures that your Board of Directors and managers have the information they need to make decisions and allocate the organization's resources. It also inspires confidence in your funders.

The people responsible for your organization's financial management need to be able to plan and budget resources (operating and capital budgets), manage cash, do accounting, and provide financial reporting. The Board of Directors and senior managers should be involved in financial management and be clear about accountability. Your organization also requires skilled people, at both the Board and the staff levels, to carry out the financial analysis and work.

Financial statements are a barometer of an organization's health. Sound internal financial procedures for administering your organization's operating funds and program grants offer assurance that monies are being directed properly.

Overall, your budget should support the important goals of your organization. For example, if international exchange of information is one of your organization's priorities, your budget should allocate the funds needed to obtain electronic-data systems, to host international visitors, and to conduct other related activities in support of this goal.

Financial management includes financial planning, financial accountability, and financial statements and systems, which will be discussed individually in this section.

Financial planning

Financial planning enables your organization to forecast its future operating revenues and expenses and its capital and equipment requirements. The ability to plan revenues provides a framework within which your organization can make decisions about programs and other expenses. This financial planning should take account of your organization's short- and long-term financial requirements.

FINANCIAL-PLANNING ISSUES

Does your organization undertake adequate financial planning to support the organization's performance?

- The organization undertakes adequate budgetary planning.
- Budget plans are timely.
- Budget plans are updated as financial information comes in.
- Members of the governing body are involved in financial planning and monitoring.
- Human resources are adequate to ensure good financial planning.
- Grants or loans are properly managed.
- Decision-making relies on monitoring and analysis of the ratio of actual to planned budgets.
- Capital and equipment forecasts are made appropriately.
- Reports are provided to senior managers, the Board of Directors, and funders on a regular basis, at least every quarter.
- Timely financial information is given to those who need it.

Financial accountability

Proper care of your organization's finances is a prerequisite for external trust. This means that your organization has appropriate checks and balances and that both internal and external professionals oversee the care of your organization's assets.

FINANCIAL-ACCOUNTABILITY ISSUES

- The auditors of the organization are satisfied with the financial managers' controls of cash and assets.
- The year-end date is clearly stated.
- The Board of Directors reviews financial statements on a regular basis.
- People on staff and the Board of Directors are competent to interpret financial information.
- Financial information is contextualized in a strategic or business plan.
- The Board of Directors establishes a committee to oversee financial issues.

Financial statements and systems

The financial managers of your organization are responsible for preparing financial statements and ensuring their integrity and objectivity. At a minimum, this means having a bookkeeping system that creates a balance sheet and an income statement. Your financial system must be able to track income, assets, and liabilities and explain expenditures. This implies the ability to control assets and liabilities and manage the cash of the organization.

FINANCIAL STATEMENTS AND SYSTEMS ISSUES

Are financial statements and systems in your organization appropriate to support its performance?

- The organization has an adequate bookkeeping system.
- The organization has adequate staff to record financial information.
- Balance sheets and income and expense statements are prepared at least quarterly.
- A procedure is in place to control and record the assets of the organization.
- Cash-flow statements are prepared.
- Cash is managed to allow the organization to benefit from a surplus and minimize the costs of cash shortages.

Infrastructure

Infrastructure comprises the basic conditions (facilities and technology) for work to go on in your organization, such as reasonable space in a building equipped with adequate lighting, clean water, and a dependable supply of electricity. Transportation to and from work is also part of this infrastructure. In developed countries with the wealth and the government structure to support adequate infrastructure, these conditions are often taken for granted. In some developing countries, ensuring adequate infrastructure is a problem organizations need to assess.

Each organization has its own infrastructural assets and liabilities. If your organization has its basic infrastructure in place, this topic will represent a small component of your assessment. If your infrastructure is debilitated, however, with water and electricity problems, then infrastructure will become a major concern.

Facilities

To understand your organization's capacity, you will need to consider the extent to which inadequate facilities interfere with the functions or potential functions of your organization. Although single deficiencies in one or more elements of infrastructure may not interfere with day-to-day work, at some point the work will be affected. Typically, the basis of many infrastructural problems is maintenance, which often suffers because of the lack of a recurrent budget for upkeep.

FACILITIES-INFRASTRUCTURE ISSUES

Is your organization's facilities infrastructure adequate to support the organization's performance?

- The organizational strategy identifies opportunities and constraints stemming from the facilities infrastructure.
- The buildings and internal services (for example, water, electricity) are adequate to support and facilitate daily work.
- Employees have an adequate transportation system to and from work.
- Communications systems (hardware) function at the levels required.
- An ongoing maintenance budget supports adequate maintenance systems and procedures.
- The organization effectively and efficiently manages the infrastructure, including building and equipment maintenance.
- An individual or a group within the organization is responsible for adequate planning to address ongoing infrastructure concerns.

INFRASTRUCTURE: THE SYMBOL OF AN ORGANIZATION

In one organization, whose mandate was to serve the needs of rural aboriginal communities internationally, the major strategic question was the organization's identity. As an organization concerned with aboriginal issues, should the majority of its Board of Directors be aboriginal? Should it seek sources of funding specifically for aboriginal projects? These questions were eventually transformed into strategies.

The most significant strategy was the Board of Directors' decision to relocate the head-quarters of the organization to an aboriginal reservation, despite the fact that the organization already had an adequate location (moderate cost, adequate rooms, etc.). For symbolic reasons and to reinforce its mission statement, it moved. So, although infrastructure was not in itself an issue, a gap existed between the infrastructure and the image that the organization wanted to project.

Technology

The technological resources of your organization comprise the equipment, machinery, and systems (including library systems, information systems, hardware, and software) that enable it to function. It is important to keep in mind that the instruments of technology are merely tools for enhancing services and products: ideas must inspire the technology.

TECHNOLOGY ISSUES

To what extent do technological resources affect your organization's performance?

- Technological planning in the organization is adequate.
- Overall, the organization's level of technology is appropriate to carry out the organization's functions.
- No one unit is seriously lagging behind the others in the level of technology needed to carry out its work.
- Access to international information is provided to all units through library and information-management systems.
- Adequate systems and training are in place to manage the organization's technology.
- Adequate information technologies are in place to manage the organization.

LINKING FACILITIES AND TECHNOLOGY

In one educational organization, one of the strategic questions concerned the organization's inadequate space. Students were dissatisfied with the size of classrooms or facilities, and the management group responsible for the 5-year plan identified the need for additional space and new classrooms.

However, after consulting a technology specialist, the organization modified its approach. The specialist advised that 5–10 years down the road, approaches to learning could be quite different. With the rise of multimedia, the classroom might not be the primary location for learning in 5 year's time. Therefore, their strategies had to be creative to ensure adequate space in the short term but without putting substantial funds into building classrooms that might not be required in 5 years.

In this case, to develop a good strategy, the organization had to analyze both the external environment (how learning technology was evolving) and the organization's capacity.

Program management

Your organization's ongoing programs, services, and products constitute its central endeavour. Indeed, they are the organization's main attempts to operationalize its mission. The function of program management is to develop and administer these programs in ways that support this mission.

Program management is vital to all other areas of organizational capacity. Ultimately, the strength of your organization's strategic leadership, human resources, financial resources, infrastructure, process management, and intra-institutional linkages affects the quality of your programs. Program performance is highly visible outside the organization and is often the major focus of organizational assessments.

Good program management requires a cycle of careful planning, implementation, and monitoring and evaluation. All programs go through this cycle, either formally or informally. Each of these aspects of good program management is discussed in this section.

Program planning

Program planning requires thinking ahead. It involves the following questions: What are our objectives? What must be done to meet these objectives? Who will do this? How will they do it? How long will it take? How much will it cost? How will we know whether we have met our objectives? And so forth.

Program planning has many levels. However, when conducting a self-assessment, you will need to determine the extent to which your organization's plans are well communicated and used as management tools. This will require written plans.

PLANNING ISSUES

To what extent does your organization appropriately plan its programs?

- Each program area and each major project has a written plan.
- Program and project plans are linked to the organization's mission.
- The organization undertakes adequate program-planning and budget-programing activities to ensure that its programs support its mission.
- The organization's programs and projects are consistent with its mission, needs, strategies, and priorities.
- Program planning takes into account technological, economic, gender, social, and environmental aspects to ensure the applicability of programs.
- Programs are given adequate timelines.
- Programs have adequate budgets.
- Program planning includes an adequate analysis of roles and responsibilities.
- A procedure is outlined to monitor results.

Implementation

The real work of managers is in making the organization's program plans work. It is all well and good to have a great plan — making it work is the hard part. Program implementation requires the organization to have people on staff who can put their skills to work. It requires integration of the management skills needed to allocate resources and the technical skills needed to do what needs to be done (for example, to provide health services and do research). Program implementation is the stage at which your organization integrates all its resources to concretely achieve its goals.

IMPLEMENTATION ISSUES

To what extent does your organization appropriately implement its programs?

- Staff support the organization's efforts to get programs accomplished and to get products and services to clients and beneficiaries.
- The staff members providing products and services have good relations with each other.
- Staff members work together to provide good products and services.
- The program team has good problem-solving skills.
- Health and safety for staff and clients are always a priority in implementation.
- Resources are efficiently used to provide the product or service.
- Schedules are adhered to in a reasonable fashion.
- Staff members are motivated to work together to get things done.
- Program meetings are productive.

Monitoring and evaluation

Programs or projects are central to the life of your organization. Management needs to keep track of programs to ensure that they are meeting their objectives and achieving their intended results. Monitoring and evaluation systems need to be built into programs and projects during their planning stage (see also "Program planning," p. 75).

MONITORING AND EVALUATION ISSUES

To what extent does your organization appropriately monitor and evaluate its programs?

- Monitoring and evaluation systems are in place.
- Program staff receive feedback on program performance.
- The monitoring and evaluation process includes adequate opportunities to clarify roles and responsibilities.
- The process includes adequate opportunities to review program indicators to measure progress against plans.
- Timelines are monitored to reduce overruns.
- Budgets are reviewed in a timely fashion.
- Programs are reviewed on a regular basis to determine how well they contribute to the organization's overall strategy.
- Drawing lessons is encouraged.
- Corrective actions are taken when difficulties arise.
- Staff members see monitoring and evaluation as ongoing and normal processes.

Organizational processes

Organizational processes are part of your organization's dynamic. These processes are major components of both stability and change. In the context of a self-assessment, it is important to examine four processes: planning; problem-solving and decision-making; communications; and monitoring and evaluation. Each of these processes is discussed in this section. It is important to consider the nature of these processes and their impacts on your organization's performance.

Planning

Planning helps your organization predict how its members will behave. Your strategic plan sets the overall direction; operational planning is the process by which that strategy is translated into specific objectives and methodologies to accomplish your goals. This involves making the best use of resources of time and people (for example, developing timelines and schedules).

PLANNING ISSUES

To what extent does the your organization's planning process contribute to its performance?

- Planning, policy, and procedure development occur in the organization at all levels, from the governing board to departments and individual projects.
- The process of planning contributes to the strategic direction of the organization.
- Plans are clear, and they provide adequate direction for the organization's members.
- Plans, policies, and procedures are generally followed.
- Planning is part of the organization's culture.
- Staff members feel that they are involved in planning.
- Planning is linked to monitoring and evaluation.

Problem-solving and decision-making

Problem-solving and decision-making interact and reinforce each other. Both processes must function well at every level of your organization. These processes include the ability to define important problems, gather the data to understand the issue, create a set of alternatives for dealing with a problem, decide on solutions, create the conditions to carry out decisions, and monitor these decisions and the problem's resolution. Timeliness is a key element in these processes.

Do the problem-solving and decision-making processes support your organization in carrying out its functions?

- The implementation of work flows smoothly at every level of the organization.
- Decisions are timely.
- Performance gaps and opportunities are identified quickly enough to resolve them to the benefit of the individuals involved and the productivity of the organization.
- Problem-solving and decision-making mechanisms are in place.
- People on the governing board and within the ranks of senior managers have adequate organizational problem-solving and decision-making skills.
- Problem-solving and decision-making are adequate in departments and for important projects.
- The staff members feel empowered by the problem-solving and decision-making processes.
- The staff members try to solve problems before they become big concerns.

Communication

The function of internal communications in your organization is to exchange information and achieve a shared understanding among staff members. Internal communications can serve as the glue holding an organization together or it can break it apart, because both information and misinformation flow constantly in organizations.

Accurate information helps keep your organization's employees informed and motivated: aside from the specific information they need to carry out their work, the organization's members also need information to make them feel that they are part of an important effort and work for a wider purpose. Your organization needs mechanisms to help staff members obtain both types of information. Coordinating committees, newsletters, and meetings of various sorts all provide vehicles for transmitting correct messages.

Monitoring and evaluation

Organizational monitoring and evaluation complement program evaluation and monitoring. Organizational monitoring can help clarify your program objectives, link activities and inputs to those objectives, set performance targets, collect routine data, and feed results directly to those responsible. Organizational monitoring is an ongoing, systematic process of self-assessment.

COMMUNICATION ISSUES

Is your organization's performance effectively supported by its communication system?

- People in the organization feel there is adequate, ongoing communication about the organization's activities.
- Staff members receive information about the organization's mission and its progress in fulfilling the mission.
- Information circulated in the organization about activities is rarely distorted.
- Mechanisms are in place to correct rumours.
- People have easy access to others they must deal with in the organization and can easily communicate with them.
- Written communication is adequate.
- Meetings are viewed as productive ways of communicating.
- Adequate use is made of communication technology.
- Two-way communication is encouraged.
- Multichannel communication is often used.
- Listening is valued.
- Cultural diversity is a consideration in communicating with others.

Organizational evaluation looks at why and how overall results were or were not achieved. It links specific activities to overall results, includes broader outcomes that are not readily quantifiable, explores unintended results, and provides overall lessons that can help your organization to adjust programs and policies to improve results.

MONITORING AND EVALUATION ISSUES

Is your organization's monitoring and evaluation adequate to improve performance?

- Policies and procedures are in place to guide evaluation and monitoring.
- Resources are assigned to monitoring and evaluation.
- Monitoring and evaluation are valued at all levels in the organization, as ways to improve performance.
- The organization obtains and uses data to monitor and evaluate its units and activities.
- Use is made of data gathered through the organization's overall monitoring and evaluation activities.
- The organization has an evaluation plan or performance-monitoring framework.
- Strategy, program, policy, and budgetary documents mention evaluation results.
- People have the skills to perform monitoring and evaluation.
- Monitoring and evaluation processes are valued.
- The organization learns lessons from monitoring and evaluation and makes changes as a result.

Interinstitutional linkages

Having regular contact with other institutions, organizations, and groups with strategic importance to your organization can result in a healthy exchange of approaches and resources (including knowledge and expertise). Your organization may be forming linkages or may already have linkages with potential collaborators and collegial bodies, potential funders, or key constituents.

Linkages help your organization keep up with advances in pertinent fields and give your organization access to wide-ranging sources of up-to-date information within each area of your organization's work.

Today, many types of linkages can and need to be made to support your organization's performance. For example, new information technologies can help your organization to learn about the most recent approaches to programing and managerial issues. They also bring new ways to communicate with potential allies and collaborators in key program and funding areas. Two aspects of interinstitutional linkages are discussed in this section: relationships such as networks, joint ventures, partnerships, and coalitions and electronic linkages.

Networks, joint ventures, partnerships, and coalitions

At the same time as electronic linkages are opening organizations to new ideas and ways of communicating, a similar revolution is occurring with respect to new organizational patterns that support joint work and collaboration.

Many organizations are finding that they are unable to make progress in achieving their missions without the support of similar organizations. Many are forming new types of relationship (either formal or informal) with other organizations to support their objectives.

Networks are informal linkages, groups loosely coupled to serve common interests. The new and joint ventures, partnerships, and coalitions are more formal. The most formal of these relationships are based on contractual agreements. All of these new linkages are breaking down the boundaries of organizations and are changing the way they operate.

NETWORK, JOINT-VENTURE, PARTNERSHIP, AND COALITION ISSUES

Has your organization established or pursued external linkages adequate to support the organization's performance?

- The organization has adequate formal and informal linkages with like-minded organizations.
- Institutional linkages are adequately supported.
- Institutional linkages contribute efficiently to the organization's goals and mission.
- Fruitful, ongoing partnerships with external organizations through these linkages bring new ideas or resources, or both, to the organization.
- The organization is using these linkages to communicate information about its work to external stakeholders, including the general public.

Electronic linkages

Organizational capacity and performance can be increased if an organization makes appropriate use of new electronic technologies. These new technologies can improve your organization's communications and keep people informed about the latest ideas. The organization's members can join Internet discussion groups, listservs, and other electronic mechanisms that link people with like minds and ideas. Electronic systems give your organization an opportunity to search the entire globe for new ideas and information.

ELECTRONIC-LINKAGE ISSUES

Has your organization established or pursued electronic linkages adequate to support its performance?

- The organization is electronically linked to the outside world of colleagues, clients, and markets (users) to make these relationships active and beneficial.
- Electronic networks are financially and technically supported.
- Electronic networks effectively respond to the needs, shared interests, and capabilities of the organization.
- Electronic networks support new efficient practices.
- Fruitful, ongoing partnerships with external organizations through electronic linkages bring new ideas or resources, or both, to the organization.
- The organization is using electronic linkages to communicate information about its work to external stakeholders, including the general public.

EXERCISE 12. Examining organizational capacity

Instructions: This exercise can help you begin identifying capacity gaps affecting overall performance in the organization. You might want to conduct this exercise with a group of senior managers, organization members, and the self-assessment team.

Using the chart below as a guide, reflect on the capacities of your organization. Identify capacity gaps and how they affect your organization's performance. Discuss the seriousness of these issues with the self-assessment team and see if there is some consensus on the priority issues.

Capacity issue	How the issue affects the performance of the organization	Seriousness		
		High	Med.	Low
Strategic leadership [Example] The Board of Directors not sufficiently involved in our work.	[Example] Funders question the extent to which the organization is truly a member-driven organization; thus, it hurts our financial sustainable.		✔	
Human resources				
Financial resources				
Infrastructure				
Program management				
Process management				
Interinstitutional linkages				

EXERCISE 13. Summarizing the performance issues

Instructions: Before you collect and analyze your data, you might find it useful to summarize your performance issues. Using the matrix below as a guide, summarize the major performance issues you have already identified and then develop the key questions and subquestions for each issue.

Major issue	Key questions	Subquestions
[Example] Relevance to stakeholders	[Example] To what extent is our organization relevant to its stakeholders?	[Example] Have we experienced changes in the level of satisfaction of our stakeholders in the last year? Have the number, needs, priorities of our stakeholders changed over the last year? Have we adapted (or added) new services and programs in response to the demands of our major stakeholders? Are we monitoring sufficiently the changing demands of our stakeholders and their levels of satisfaction?
Efficiency		

A P P E N D I X   I

Tools for Self-Assessment

. . . .

TOOL 1

THE FIVE-EASY-PIECES MODEL
FOR A QUICK SELF-ASSESSMENT

. . . .

The five-easy-pieces model is an approach to self-assessment that your organization might like to try. Using this model is one way we have been able to begin a relatively quick and easy discussion:

1. Identify key performance issues in your organization

2. Map these issues against efficiency, effectiveness, relevance, and financial sustainability.

3. Describe where you are now.

4. Diagnose your performance against environment, motivation, and capacity.

5. Prescribe what to keep and what to change.

TOOL 2
STAKEHOLDER ASSESSMENT

Purpose

The purpose of this tool is to help you identify stakeholders and their interest in the organization. It can be used to analyze organizational relevance and assess the environment.

Instructions

1. Fill in the names of your stakeholders in the first column (see Exercise 3 [mapping the stakeholders] in Chapter 1, p. 9).

2. Identify each stakeholder's category. These might be funders, employees, senior leadership, or the organization's partners. You should customize your categories to suit your organization's identified stakeholders. You might also indicate whether a stakeholder

    - Is an integral part of the organization;
    - Is interested in, and committed to, the organization;
    - Knows the organization but is not committed to it; or
    - Has a vested interest in destroying the organization, that is, competitors. etc.

3. Indicate each stakeholder's interest in the self-assessment results, that is, whether a stakeholder

    - Will use the results for planning;
    - Will use them to support the organization; or
    - Will use the assessment to design new programs, introduce change, or develop future strategies, etc.

        Each stakeholder may have several interests.

4. Identify each stakeholder's possible participation or role in the self-assessment, that is, whether the stakeholder can

    - Be a data or information provider;
    - Make a decision on the self-assessment findings; or
    - Become a beneficiary of change arising from the assessment, etc.

Each stakeholder may have several roles in the assessment. These can be listed using the following table format:

STAKEHOLDER	CATEGORY	INTERESTS	PARTICIPATION OR ROLE

TOOL 3

PERFORMANCE-ISSUES WORKSHEET

· ·

Purpose

The purpose of this worksheet is to provide an analytical tool to help organizations to understand the relationship between performance and the factors that support performance. It can be used at any stage in the diagnostic process at which the team attempts to identify the causes of good or poor performance. It is an evolving tool that can be updated as performance factors emerge.

· ·

Instructions

Use the following worksheet to help you identify the possible underlying causes of performance issues:

PERFORMANCE ISSUE	FACTORS IN THE ENVIRONMENT THAT AFFECT THIS ISSUE	ASPECTS OF ORGANIZATIONAL MOTIVATION THAT AFFECT THIS ISSUE	ASPECTS OF ORGANIZATIONAL CAPACITY THAT AFFECT THIS ISSUE

TOOL 4
CULTURE AUDIT

. . . .

Purpose

The purpose of the culture audit is to provide the assessment team with a list of areas within which data can be gathered respecting organizational motivation. The assessment team can use it to help in planning data collection. Some of the questions could be used in animating focus groups with staff members or people on the Board of Directors – to take the pulse of the organization.

. . . .

Instructions

Part 1– Individually answer as many of the questions below as you can.

Part 2 – In a group, discuss your answers and whether one can answer all the questions. Are most people agreed on their answers?

---

1. What kind of people are involved in this organization? Who are the real leaders? Who gets ahead? (These questions provide information on the informal reward and power system, as well as identifying any heroes.)

2. What is it like to be part of this organization? (This question provides a real overview of the organization's culture.)

3. Why is the organization successful? (This helps describe what areas are perceived as important.)

4. Can you clearly define the organization's values or beliefs and norms of acceptable behaviour?

5. What is the organization's culture now? How strongly and uniformly does this exist across the organization?

6. Is the organization a safe environment in which to grow and make mistakes?

7. Are people considered important to this organization?

8. What skills and actions are rewarded?

9. Does the leadership promote openness, risk-taking, and trust?

10. What is the history of the organization?

11. Does the organization focus inwardly, rather than to the outside world, that is, does it have only a short-term focus?

12. How frequent is the turnover of personnel?

13. What are the "war stories" and anecdotes of this organization?

14. What are the major events in this organization's past?

15. How do people new to the organization learn the ropes?

16. What matters have a high priority in this organization? What matters have a low priority?

17. Overall, how would you describe the culture of your organization?

TOOL 5
WORK BREAKDOWN

Purpose

The purpose of this form is to provide a planning tool for the assessment team. In the phase column, we sometimes place dates as well as phases. The other columns identify the tasks or activities to be completed, the results or outputs of those activities, the timing planned for the activity, and the persons responsible for these activities. The tasks and activities can be either broad or very specific.

PHASE	TASK OR ACTIVITY	OUTPUT	MILESTONE	RESPONSIBLE TEAM MEMBER
I	Plan self-assessment	Matrix	May 1	Georges
	Develop budget	Budget	May 1	Pablo
	Develop data-collection instruments	Questionnaire	May 18	Rosalie
		Focus-group protocols	May 27	Georges
		Interview protocols	May 27	Georges
II	Collect data	Questionnaire data	Jul 15	Rosalie
		Focus-group report	Jun 30	Georges
		Interview data	Jun 30	Georges
		Document review	Jun 15	Pablo
III	Analyze data	Questionnaire	Aug 1	Rosalie
		Focus group	Aug 1	Georges
		Interview	Aug 1	Georges
		Document	Aug 1	Pablo
IV	Reporting	Draft	Aug 15	Rosalie
		Briefing	Aug 18	Rosalie and Georges
		Final	Aug 30	Rosalie
V	Management			Georges

PHASE	TASK OR ACTIVITY	OUTPUT	MILESTONE	RESPONSIBLE TEAM MEMBER
I				
II				
III				
IV				
V				

TOOLS

TIPS

QUESTIONNAIRES

EXERCISES

TOOL 6

PERSON–DAY ANALYSIS

. . . .

Purpose

The purpose of this form is to provide a planning tool for the self-assessment team. With this tool, each member of the team is assigned responsibilities for specific tasks and an estimate is made of the time it might take to complete the task assigned. This tool should be used early in the assessment phase to allow the organization to begin to assess the resources the self-assessment will require.

ACTIVITY	TEAM MEMBER 1	TEAM MEMBER 2	TEAM MEMBER 3	TOTAL
1. Work planning				
Assessment framework				
Methodology				
Data-collection instruments				
Budget				
Report outline				
2. Data collection				
Document review				
Focus groups				
Interviews				
Questionnaire surveys				
3. Data analysis				
Development of frameworks				
Analysis of interview or focus-group data				
Analysis of questionnaire data				
Analysis of project or organizational data				
Formulating findings and conclusions				
Validating analysis with key stakeholders				
4. Reporting				
Drafting report				
Briefings				
Revising final report				
5. Process management				
Coordination				
Financial management				
Total days				

Tips for Designing Data-Collection Instruments

. . . .

Purpose

The purpose of this collection of tips is to improve the ability of your assessment team to create data-collection instruments and to collect data. It provides advice on the development of instruments, data-collection methods and data analysis for group techniques, questionnaires, and interviews – three common data-collection approaches. If considered at the planning stage, these tips will help your team determine which type of data collection is appropriate for addressing each key issue.

. . . .

TOOLS

TIPS

QUESTIONNAIRES

EXERCISES

TIP 1

GROUP TECHNIQUES

The following list provides an overview of the procedure:

- Define the purpose [not discussed below]
- Develop the questions
- Develop a guide
- Arrange a schedule
- Set up the groups
- Conduct the sessions
- Record the data
- Analyze the data
- Present the findings [not discussed below]

Develop the questions

Plan for 5–10 questions. Effective group questions are carefully defined. They

- Are always open ended (none of these are to be yes-or-no questions);
- Are qualitative rather than quantitative in orientation (they ask about perceptions and feelings, rather than about facts or numbers);
- Never ask "why" directly;
- Have many imbedded probes; and
- Allow for process concerns as well as content.

Develop a guide

Successful groups for data collection comprise people who

- Share some common characteristic (such as being your client);
- Have diverse experiences (intact groups don't work);
- Represent diverse perspectives; and
- Number between 6 and 12 people.

Arrange a schedule

- Allow 2 hours per group;
- Give no breaks; and
- Don't fill time (session ends when you have extracted the data).

Set up the groups

- Arrange seating in a circle for good eye contact; and
- Position moderator and assistant moderator or recorder at opposite ends of the seating arrangement – for a different perspective.

Conduct the sessions

Content
Opening

- Introductions
- Clarify duration of session
- Clarify guidelines
  - Keep responses confidential; and
  - Encourage positive and negative perspectives.

Major questions

- Ask questions according to your guide; and
- Use probes.

Questions to ask yourself

- What else do I need to ask to understand this person's perspective?
- Am I hearing everything I need to understand?
- What does all this mean when seen collectively?
- How do I bring out real feelings?
- How much time is left?

Summary

- Summarize the main points that emerged; and
- Perhaps ask an overall wrap-up question, such as "Is the program generally effective?"

Conclusion

- Thank the group for their participation;
- Let people in the group know what the next steps in the process will be.

Technique

What to do

- Be innocent and empathetic;
- Engage in active listening, paraphrasing, and summarizing;
- Exert control without leading;
- Balance contributions of the dominant and silent participants;
- Ask if anyone sees any matter differently; and
- Use pauses and probes effectively.

What to avoid

- Head nodding (except on an exceptional basis); and
- Agreeing ("OK," "Yes").

How to draw people out

- Begin with a broad question, such as "What did you think of … ?";
- Ask for the opinions of participants who have not yet responded; and
- Use silence – ask a question and then take enough time to look around at the group for responses.

How to cut off talkers

- Stop long-winded arguments by restating the two opinions and then asking other participants for any different perspectives on the issue;
- Use the "Cop" – hold up your palm to stop someone;
- Pat the arm of a big talker next to you;
- Avoid eye contact with a dominant talker;
- Try saying "How about letting someone else go first?," "Hold that thought, we haven't heard from Joe yet," "Yes, you already mentioned that," or "I get the feeling that others would like to be heard"; and
- Create a major distraction and then restart the discussion.

Record the data

Tape-recording

- Advantage – a complete record is made of the data.
- Disadvantage – it is time-consuming to listen to the tape.

Techniques

- Inform the participants and obtain permission;
- Use an unobtrusive recording device; and
- Use tapes long enough not to have to change tapes in the middle of the discussion.

Written record

- Notes should be taken even if the session is tape-recorded;
- Make a note of the tape position (counter) from time to time in the margin of your notes, so that specific points can be located easily on the tape;
- Notes should be taken by an assistant moderator, not the moderator;
- Make notes continuously, to avoid giving cues to participants about the value of their contributions;
- Underline points that seem to be significant; and
- You might predefine categories and organize a page of your notebook to accommodate comments in the anticipated categories.

Observer comments

- Make notes on things you think of during the session: important themes, ideas for the next group session, rephrasing of questions, etc. Identify these as your thoughts.

Analyze the data

Steps

1. Type up significant commentary from the rough notes and record the speakers' names if possible.

2. Cut and paste comments into themes (with a computer or scissors).

3. Order the comments within the themes into subthemes.

4. Arrange the themes in order of importance.

5. Edit the themes

   - To eliminate redundancy;
   - To ensure comments are not one person's perspective only; and
   - To create a balanced, accurate reflection of what was actually said.

6. Write a summary statement for each theme.

7. Select and edit actual quotations to illustrate each theme, but

   - Avoid extreme views;
   - Select statements that are typical;
   - Correct grammar and language usage where required; and
   - Conceal the identities of participants by removing names and identifying details.

 SEE TIP 4 – Basis for Judgement (p. 112)

TIP 2
INTERVIEWS

Whether interviews are conducted face to face or over the telephone, following certain procedures can help you to get the most out of them. These procedures are as follows:

- Determine the approach
- Determine general and specific research questions
- Draft the interview questions
- Pilot test the protocol
- Arrange a schedule of interviews [not discussed below]
- Prepare to record the responses
- Conduct the interviews
- Analyze interview data

Determine the approach

Your first step in using interviews is to decide what approach to use:

- *Key-informant interview* – A key-informant interview is designed to collect data from an individual who is unique by virtue of position or experience (for example, a department head, who can represent a whole department).
- *Normative interview* – A normative interview is used to collect information from large numbers of clients (for example, by interviewing typical, individual clients).

The type of interview will determine your plan:

- *Interview guide* – A general set of questions used in an elite interview; or
- *Interview protocol* – A highly structured instrument resembling a question- naire. (The interviewer often records the answers on the protocol.)

Determine general and specific research questions

- What do you need to find out?
- What information is it essential for you to obtain from the interview? (Remember, this may be your only chance to get the information.)

Draft the interview questions

- Some questions may be open ended, that is,
  - Ask for general information; or
  - Don't restrict the answer, for example, "How do you feel about ... ."
- Some questions may be closed, that is,
  - Ask for specific information; or
  - Restrict interviewee to factual answers, yes-or-no responses, or a multiple choice.

Sequence the questions

- Organize the questions in sections concerning major themes.

Consider your process needs

- Prepare suitable transitions from one topic to the next;
- Prepare probes and process questions; and
- Remind yourself to summarize.

Prepare introductory and concluding statements for the client

- Purpose of the interview, its duration, and its confidentiality;
- The value of the client's contribution; and
- Follow-up.

Pilot test the protocol

It is important to do a trial run of any interview. This pilot test will help you to validate

- The content of your questions;
- The flow of topics;
- The recording technique; and
- The timing.

If you are using other interviewers, you will need several training sessions to ensure that they learn to use the protocol.

Revise your interview protocol or guide after you pilot test it with clients or train other interviewers.

Telephone interviews

- Use these for normative interviews;
- Use these for elite interviews if you can't meet in person;
- Arrange time in advance – state purpose, scope, and time required; and
- For a key-informant interview conducted by telephone, fax the main questions and themes from the interview guide in advance.

Face-to-face interviews

- Give priority to this method for elite interviews;
- Arrange time and place;
- Ask that calls and other interruptions be held; and
- Meet where you can really discuss issues.

Arrange a schedule of interviews

Prepare to record the responses

- Decide on a general method for recording the interview: tape-recording, writing notes;
- Organize a protocol for written responses; and
- Plan to record verbal statements and to note nonverbal communication.

Conduct the interviews

It is important that you, as an interviewer, maintain control of the process as well as of the content of the interview.

Control the content

- By planning; and
- By following the protocol or guide.

Control the process

- By starting on the right foot – a good introduction establishes a good tone, reviews the overall agenda for the interview, and sets a time limit;
- By cutting off answers that go on too long;
- By keeping on track – leading client back to your protocol questions;
- By encouraging responses from more reserved interviewees
  - Through the use of humour, and
  - Through being willing to wait in silence; and
- By using effective communication techniques:
  - Active listening;
  - Openness and empathy;
  - Paraphrasing; and
  - Summarizing.

Analyze interview data

Normative interviews

- Quantitative responses can be recorded and statistically analyzed; and
- Qualitative responses can be analyzed for content.

Key-informant interviews

With key-informant interviews, you are trying to understand the answers
to such questions as

- What are the key views of this group of clients?
- Which issues can we do something about?
- Which ones are beyond our control?
- Which views are shared by most members of this group?
- Which views differ?
- Why do some views differ? Is it the individual personality or the role,
  position, or perspective of the person?

Some views may need to be weighted for importance; for example, some
clients may be more important than others, either because they are bigger
clients or because their needs are more vital. The bottom-line question is what
do our elite clients feel about our goods and services. What does this tell us?

SEE TIP 4 – Basis for Judgement (p. 112)

Tips on asking questions

Interviewers often get into trouble because they violate basic rules.
The following problems should be avoided:

TYPE	EXAMPLE	WHAT TO DO OR AVOID
Double-barreled questions	Have you ever experienced burnout, and what do you do to prevent it?	Avoid double-barreled questions. Ask one question at a time. Do not combine questions and expect an answer.
Two-in-one questions	What are the advantages and disadvantages of working at this university?	Do not combine opposite positions in one question. Separate out the parts, and things will be much clearer.
Restrictive questions	Do you think that female administrators are as good as male administrators?	The phraseology of this question eliminates the possibility that females might be better. Avoid questions that inherently eliminate some options.
Leading questions	ABC Inc. wants departments to be close to their clients. What do you think of my department's client relations?	Do not precede questions with a position statement. In this type of question, the interviewer states a view or summarizes the position of a current or recent event and then asks for a response. This tends to lead the respondent in a given direction.
Loaded questions	Would you favour or oppose murder by agreeing with a woman's free choice concerning abortion?	Avoid questions that use loaded words and are emotionally charged.

TIP 3

QUESTIONNAIRES

The following procedures are recommended for a questionnaire survey:

- Determine the major questions
- Draft questionnaire items
- Design the questionnaire
- Pilot test the questionnaire
- Develop a data-collection strategy
- Develop a cover letter and send the questionnaire
- Monitor the response
- Analyze the survey data

Determine the major questions

You should begin by understanding the major questions or issues you wish to address. These will generally be reflected in the questionnaire sections, as described below.

Typical sections

Introduction or background information

This section includes questions about your client that may be important to your analysis. It should solicit background information you need to address, such as the respondent's department, region, experience, gender, position, and experience with the supplier.

Ask only what is essential to your subanalyses. If you don't need to know, don't ask.

Quality of goods or services received by your client

This section is the heart of the questionnaire and requires you to develop dimensions of quality that may be important. The client (respondent) then rates the quality of your outputs along these dimensions.

Other considerations

For this section, choose a title that matches other important dimensions of client service, such as "Timeliness of Delivery," "Safety," or "Environmental Responsibility."

Responsiveness, problem-solving, and client service

This set of questions will address your client's perceptions of your service. This section might be merged with the quality or other-considerations section.

These major sections of your questionnaire provide the overall outline. Once you know these major themes, you need to develop actual questions or items.

Draft questionnaire items

Types of questionnaire items

You must draft actual questionnaire items within each of the sections of your questionnaire. It is difficult to vary the types of questions too often, so economize within each section by asking similar types of questions.

You will need to master six types of questionnaire item before you invent your own. Unproved alternatives are often confusing to the reader. So use unproved alternatives only after you are fully familiar with the types of items described below.

Multiple-choice item

This type of question is useful for the introduction or background-information section.

How long have you been a PhD student at McGill? (Please check one.)
☐ Less than 6 months   ☐ 1–2 years   ☐ More than 2 years

Fill-in-the-blank item

Use this form when the possibilities are too numerous to list using a multiple-choice item. They work well in a mix with multiple-choice. So, they are also good in the introduction.

In which department do you work? _____

Rating-scale item

This type of item enables you to collect a lot of information efficiently. Rating-scale items are good for rating your goods and services, other considerations, and so forth.

How important is it for you to learn about:

	NOT AT ALL				VERY
a) Environmental responsibility	1	2	3	4	5

List item

This type of item provides a stronger form of feedback than a rating scale. It forces the client to identify what he or she considers important and helps the researcher to avoid the problem of people just agreeing because it is easy to check a box without feeling that it is important to them.

> What aspects of your training course did you like most? Please list three of them.
>
> _____
>
> _____
>
> _____
>
> _____
>
> _____

Comment-on item

This type of question is another way to gain an understanding of what your client considers important. It is particularly useful for "mopping up" in the concluding section.

> Please write any other comments about the work of school principal and suggestions for training that you consider important:
>
> _____
>
> _____
>
> _____
>
> _____
>
> _____

Likert-scale items

The Likert scale allows the respondent to agree or disagree with a series of statements. (Note, these are statements, not questions.) The Likert scale is easy to use, if you know how, and like other rating scales it is an efficient way to collect lots of information.

	STRONGLY DISAGREE	DISAGREE	NEITHER DISAGREE NOR AGREE	AGREE	STRONGLY AGREE
I am satisfied with my professional development (that is, I am acquiring new skills and knowledge)	☐	☐	☐	☐	☐
There are possibilities for career advancement (that is, for increased responsibilities)	☐	☐	☐	☐	☐

Now, you try a few. Write your own statements for dimensions of your work unit's outputs. Include items that are worded both positively and negatively.

1. _____

_____

2. _____

_____

3. _____

Design the questionnaire

As you write the items, you should begin considering an overall design for your questionnaire. Follow these rules:

- Lay out items to avoid confusion;
- Use the formats shown in the examples;
- Don't allow a question to cross over two pages;
- Instruct the respondent in what you want him or her to do for each type of question; and
- Number the questions consecutively.

Use a booklet
- To make it professional and facilitate completion.

Have a title and introductory explanation
- To let your clients know what you are doing; and
- To help them fill out the questionnaire properly.

Arrange the questionnaire in sections, each with a title
- To help structure the respondent's thinking; and
- To facilitate analysis.

Group similar types of items together
- Do this especially with rating-scale items; but
- Fill-in-the-blank and multiple-choice items can be mixed together.

Use all available space
- Try to limit the length of the questionnaire to four pages; and
- Use space for comments to fill in pages.

Pilot test the questionnaire

Even the best questionnaire needs testing. You might understand everything in the questionnaire, but your client may not. Here are some tips to help you test your questionnaire.

Show the questionnaire to critical colleagues

- Ask them to read it and to comment in the margins; and
- Revise the questionnaire.

Test the questionnaire with a few clients

- Assemble 5–6 clients;
- Ask them to complete the questionnaire in writing; and
- Discuss each question with the group.

In completing this step, ask such questions as

- Was the item clear, and could it be answered?
- Did the question hit the important aspect of the issue?
- What has been left out?
- Does the whole questionnaire enable your client to really express what he or she thinks of your organization's work?

Revise again

It sounds like a lot of work. It is! Creating a good questionnaire may take a week of full-time work, even for a professional.

Develop a data-collection strategy

Now you have a questionnaire ready to go! You'll need to work out a strategy for how and where to send it. The first part of your strategy is to select a sample of people who fairly represent all your clients. Prepare a list of your sample clients.

The second part of your strategy is to decide on the technology you will use to send out your questionnaire.

Standard

Questionnaires can be printed, in your office or by a printer, and mailed to respondents. Respondents fill them out and mail them back. Results are manually input into a database or statistical program for analysis.

Optical scanning

It is possible to print questionnaires so that they can be read by an optical scanner that picks up the responses automatically. The questionnaires in Appendix 3 were designed to be used in this way. (Note, pictographs can be used to illustrate points.)

Electronic questionnaires

The coming wave for internal client-needs assessments is the e-mail questionnaire. This is designed on a computer and sent as a computer file to clients via e-mail. The client receives the file, completes the questionnaire on his or her computer, and sends the file back to you by e-mail.

Follow-up

You also need a follow-up strategy. This may include

- Tracking the number returned each day – e-mail lets you know who hasn't yet replied;
- Sending a reminder 2 weeks after first mailing; and
- Deciding on corrective action, if returns are poor.

When key people in each unit distribute and collect the questionnaire, pyramid networks are great, but personal networks are the best of all for getting returns.

Develop a cover letter and send the questionnaire

Each client in your sample should receive

- A cover letter;
- A professionally developed questionnaire; and
- A self-addressed return envelope, unless you use e-mail.

Cover letter

Every successful questionnaire comes with a cover letter. The letter should contain six pieces of information:

- The purpose of the questionnaire;
- Who is sending it;
- Why the respondent was selected;
- Where, how, and when to return the questionnaire;
- Whom to contact if there are further questions; and
- Whether and how the results will be shared.

Monitor the response

- Count on 4 to 6 weeks to get responses to your questionnaire;
- Use your follow-up strategy: send reminder letters or put your network into action; and
- Start your analysis when responses dry up.

Analyze the survey data

Questionnaire analysis generally means dealing with large numbers or with a variety of numbers. This usually requires you to use statistical concepts and computers. Many simple statistics programs are available to help you analyze data.

 SEE TIP 4 – Basis for Judgement (p. 112)

Six steps for constructing effective questionnaires: summary

1. *Determine your questions*
   - What do you intend to find out?
   - How will the information be helpful?
   - Which issues will relate to the questionnaire?

2. *Specify your subquestions*
   - List all the things you want to find out;
   - Indicate those subquestions to be included in the questionnaire; and
   - Refine your list.

3. *Draft the items*
   - Translate questions into items; and
   - Formulate multiple-choice, fill-in-the-blank, rating-scale, list, comment-on, and Likert-scale questions.

4. *Sequence the items*
   - Group the items into topic sections;
   - Group the items by question type; and
   - Rewrite the items as necessary.

5. *Design the questionnaire*
   - Order and number questions;
   - Layout a booklet format; and
   - Arrange the questions on pages.

6. *Pilot test the questionnaire*
   - Clarify the wording of the questionnaire with respondents;
   - Group test the draft questionnaire;
   - Discuss the questionnaire with the group; and
   - Revise the questionnaire and retest it if necessary.

TIP 4

BASIS FOR JUDGMENT

Because the same data can be interpreted in different ways, it is important to take these potential differences of interpretation into account at the design stage. Three main decision-making methods are generally used to make judgments about data:

- Comparing present data with those from the organization's past, accepted industry standards, or practices that have worked well in other similar environments (norms or benchmarking);

- Reliance on an expert opinion – an expert can be someone with good insight into your organization, a practitioner in organizational development, or someone who knows your sector well; and

- Comparing organizational data with preset criteria (objectively verifiable indicators).

Your self-assessment team can use one or more of these methods to interpret the assessment data.

A P P E N D I X 3

Sample Questionnaires

. . . .

SAMPLE 1. STAFF QUESTIONNAIRE

Purpose

This questionnaire is a tool to obtain data from staff on their level of satisfaction with the organization and their perception of its level of performance.

. . . .

STAFF QUESTIONNAIRE

Are we on track? XYZ would like to find out how you feel about the organization. Please help us by answering the following questions. Do not give your name. Results will be grouped, and all individual comments will be kept anonymous.

Performance Please indicate the extent to which you agree or disagree with the following statements by putting a ✔ in the appropriate box.

		STRONGLY DISAGREE	DISAGREE	AGREE	STRONGLY AGREE	DO NOT KNOW
1.	XYZ is a pleasant place to work.	☐	☐	☐	☐	☐
2.	I have a clear idea of how XYZ sees itself in 5 years.	☐	☐	☐	☐	☐
3.	I feel my salary is competitive in comparison with those in similar international agencies.	☐	☐	☐	☐	☐
4.	I can see a long-term future for myself here.	☐	☐	☐	☐	☐
5.	I am satisfied with my benefits package.	☐	☐	☐	☐	☐
6.	XYZ does not place enough emphasis on the quality of service it provides.	☐	☐	☐	☐	☐
7.	I have a clear understanding of my objectives for this year.	☐	☐	☐	☐	☐
8.	I usually do not know what is going on in the organization.	☐	☐	☐	☐	☐
9.	XYZ values its employees.	☐	☐	☐	☐	☐
10.	XYZ's hiring policy is fair.	☐	☐	☐	☐	☐
11.	XYZ is well managed.	☐	☐	☐	☐	☐

	STRONGLY DISAGREE	DISAGREE	AGREE	STRONGLY AGREE	DO NOT KNOW
12. Female and male employees are treated equally.	☐	☐	☐	☐	☐
13. XYZ strongly supports staff training and professional development.	☐	☐	☐	☐	☐
14. I am satisfied with my work space.	☐	☐	☐	☐	☐
15. We have the leadership the organization needs to be a success.	☐	☐	☐	☐	☐
16. I believe that when my performance improves, so will my earnings.	☐	☐	☐	☐	☐
17. Staff training has a low priority.	☐	☐	☐	☐	☐
18. XYZ manages its technological resources effectively.	☐	☐	☐	☐	☐
19. I relate well to my co-workers.	☐	☐	☐	☐	☐
20. Some duplication of roles and functions occurs among program units and staff at XYZ.	☐	☐	☐	☐	☐
21. The technological resources at XYZ permit me to carry out my work efficiently and productively.	☐	☐	☐	☐	☐
22. Sufficient opportunity is given for professional advancement.	☐	☐	☐	☐	☐
23. I receive both positive and negative feedback from my supervisor.	☐	☐	☐	☐	☐
24. I understand what XYZ needs to do to achieve its goals.	☐	☐	☐	☐	☐
25. Our clients get their money's worth.	☐	☐	☐	☐	☐
26. The formal problem-solving processes at XYZ are effective.	☐	☐	☐	☐	☐
27. My supervisor treats all employees in my work unit equitably.	☐	☐	☐	☐	☐
28. My colleagues are competent, qualified professionals.	☐	☐	☐	☐	☐
29. I sometimes have difficulty communicating with other staff members.	☐	☐	☐	☐	☐
30. XYZ offers me sufficient opportunities to participate in job-related training.	☐	☐	☐	☐	☐
31. I believe that the performance-review system is fair.	☐	☐	☐	☐	☐
32. My work schedule is reasonable.	☐	☐	☐	☐	☐
33. XYZ does a good job of correcting any mistakes it makes with its clients.	☐	☐	☐	☐	☐
34. I communicate effectively with my supervisor.	☐	☐	☐	☐	☐

	STRONGLY DISAGREE	DISAGREE	AGREE	STRONGLY AGREE	DO NOT KNOW
35. The service we provide to clients could be improved.	☐	☐	☐	☐	☐
36. I support XYZ's corporate values.	☐	☐	☐	☐	☐
37. My current earnings reflect my performance.	☐	☐	☐	☐	☐
38. My supervisor(s) has (have) good people skills.	☐	☐	☐	☐	☐
38. I get adequate support for strengthening my weaknesses and building on my strengths.	☐	☐	☐	☐	☐
40. I see how I can help the organization become even more successful.	☐	☐	☐	☐	☐
41. I know what our corporate values are.	☐	☐	☐	☐	☐
42. XYZ is open to my ideas and suggestions.	☐	☐	☐	☐	☐
43. Promotions are based primarily on performance.	☐	☐	☐	☐	☐
44. I have too much work.	☐	☐	☐	☐	☐
45. I believe that XYZ is an equal-opportunity employer.	☐	☐	☐	☐	☐
46. I could earn more money doing the same job for someone else.	☐	☐	☐	☐	☐
47. XYZ helps me identify areas of training for my professional development.	☐	☐	☐	☐	☐
48. We have standard procedures that help me provide a better service to my clients.	☐	☐	☐	☐	☐
49. XYZ has management problems.	☐	☐	☐	☐	☐
50. I am proud of the work I do.	☐	☐	☐	☐	☐

What is important for XYZ's success? How important is each of the following to ensure XYZ's success?

	NOT AT ALL IMPORTANT	SLIGHTLY IMPORTANT	IMPORTANT	VERY IMPORTANT	OF UTMOST IMPORTANCE
51. Strong emphasis on innovation	☐	☐	☐	☐	☐
52. Superior delivery of service	☐	☐	☐	☐	☐
53. Significant impact on link institutions	☐	☐	☐	☐	☐
54. Regional cooperation	☐	☐	☐	☐	☐
55. Clear organizational vision	☐	☐	☐	☐	☐
56. Strong organizational values	☐	☐	☐	☐	☐

57. What suggestions would you give XYZ to improve itself under any of the above categories? (Give suggestions regarding those categories you feel strongly about.)

What is important to your job satisfaction? How important is each
of the following to your job satisfaction at XYZ?

	NOT AT ALL IMPORTANT	SLIGHTLY IMPORTANT	IMPORTANT	VERY IMPORTANT	OF UTMOST IMPORTANCE
58. Feedback on your performance	☐	☐	☐	☐	☐
59. Good employee benefits package	☐	☐	☐	☐	☐
60. Opportunities for career development within the organization	☐	☐	☐	☐	☐
61. Commitment to staff development	☐	☐	☐	☐	☐
62. Good communication throughout the organization	☐	☐	☐	☐	☐
63. Equity in the workplace	☐	☐	☐	☐	☐
64. Pleasant work environment	☐	☐	☐	☐	☐

65. What could XYZ do under any of the above categories to make you more satisfied with your job?

Your experiences Please answer the following questions. Anecdotes and descriptions of your experiences are especially encouraged. All comments will be kept anonymous.

66. Do you feel XYZ's system of feedback facilitates or hampers your performance? How?

67. How do the working relationships at XYZ (with colleagues or clients, or both) affect the quality of services the organization delivers?

68. Is the delivery of services at XYZ affected by its use of technology? How has your work been affected by XYZ's use of technology

69. Has your work ever been affected by the adequacy or inadequacy of budgetary planning at XYZ? If so, how?

Thank you for taking the time to complete this questionnaire

SAMPLE 2. DONOR QUESTIONNAIRE

Purpose

This questionnaire is a tool to obtain data from donors on their level of satisfaction with the organization and their perception of its level of performance.

DONOR QUESTIONNAIRE

Are we on track? XYZ would like to find out how you feel about the organization. Please help us by answering the following questions. Do not give your name. Results will be grouped, and all individual comments will be kept anonymous.

Performance Please indicate the extent to which you agree or disagree with the following statements by putting a ✔ in the appropriate box.

	STRONGLY DISAGREE	DISAGREE	AGREE	STRONGLY AGREE	DO NOT KNOW
1. XYZ's mandate is clear to me.	☐	☐	☐	☐	☐
2. I have a clear idea how XYZ sees itself developing over the next 5 years.	☐	☐	☐	☐	☐
3. XYZ's staff is of a high professional calibre.	☐	☐	☐	☐	☐
4. XYZ's location is appropriate for its mandate.	☐	☐	☐	☐	☐
5. Regional representation in XYZ is an important aspect of its work.	☐	☐	☐	☐	☐
6. XYZ does not place enough emphasis on the quality of service it provides.	☐	☐	☐	☐	☐
7. XYZ responds quickly to our requests.	☐	☐	☐	☐	☐
8. XYZ builds regional cooperation.	☐	☐	☐	☐	☐
9. XYZ is seen as a regional leader in integrated rural development.	☐	☐	☐	☐	☐
10. In our experience, XYZ's reports meet our requirements.	☐	☐	☐	☐	☐
11. XYZ is well managed.	☐	☐	☐	☐	☐
12. XYZ plans its projects well.	☐	☐	☐	☐	☐
13. XYZ professionally monitors projects.	☐	☐	☐	☐	☐
14. XYZ builds the capacities of its national link organizations.	☐	☐	☐	☐	☐
15. XYZ is innovative in its approach to rural development.	☐	☐	☐	☐	☐
16. XYZ provides good value for money.	☐	☐	☐	☐	☐
17. XYZ can adapt appropriately when required.	☐	☐	☐	☐	☐

	STRONGLY DISAGREE	DISAGREE	AGREE	STRONGLY AGREE	DO NOT KNOW
18. XYZ's mandate is in line with our organization's direction.	☐	☐	☐	☐	☐
19. XYZ's services are in an increasing demand.	☐	☐	☐	☐	☐

What is important to XTZ's success? How important is each
of the following to ensuring XYZ's success?

	NOT AT ALL IMPORTANT	SLIGHTLY IMPORTANT	IMPORTANT	VERY IMPORTANT	OF UTMOST IMPORTANCE
20. Strong emphasis on innovation	☐	☐	☐	☐	☐
21. Superior delivery of service	☐	☐	☐	☐	☐
22. Significant impact on link institutions	☐	☐	☐	☐	☐
23. Regional cooperation	☐	☐	☐	☐	☐
24. Clear organizational vision	☐	☐	☐	☐	☐
25. Strong organizational values	☐	☐	☐	☐	☐

26. What suggestions would you give XYZ to improve itself under any of the above categories? (Give suggestions regarding those categories you feel strongly about.)

_____

_____

_____

Your experiences Please answer the following questions. Anecdotes and descriptions of your experiences are especially encouraged. All comments will be kept anonymous.

27. What do you feel are XYZ's strengths?

_____

28. What are XYZ's weaknesses?

_____

29. In what areas might you be interested in working with XYZ in the future?

_____

30. In your opinion, how does XYZ rate in comparison with other regional agencies?

☐ Excellent   ☐ Good   ☐ Fair   ☐ Poor

31. Please feel free to make additional comments below:

_____

_____

_____

Thank you for taking the time to complete this questionnaire

SAMPLE 3. COVER LETTER FOR DONOR QUESTIONNAIRE

Purpose

This sample cover letter can be attached to the questionnaire going out to donors.

[Date]
[Donor name]
[Donor address]

Dear _____,

As part of our efforts to build our capacity and improve our services, XYZ is presently undergoing an organizational self-assessment and strategy-development exercise. Supported by **[donor name]**, this process will also facilitate our strategic-planning efforts. We are asking our donors to take about 10–15 minutes to complete the enclosed questionnaire. Please return it in the self-addressed, postage-paid envelope at your earliest convenience. We would appreciate your response by **[date]**, as the questionnaire is an important part of our data-collection process. All responses will be treated confidentially.

Sincerely,

[Your name]

A P P E N D I X 4

Sample Self-Assessment Exercises

. . . .

Purpose

This set of short exercises can be used at a miniretreat to encourage staff members to identify the organization's level of performance. Each of the exercises can be done separately, although when they are done as a set they provide a holistic assessment of the organization – from where it is now to where it wishes to be. The exercises also help to identify what needs to be done to bridge any gap between the organization's reality and its vision of the future. The self-assessment team can give these exercises, or this can be done with the help of someone outside the organization.

. . . .

Note the following:

- Exercise A1 ("Who is XYZ?") can be used to develop a common understanding of the organization's strengths and weaknesses. The questionnaire is completed as an individual and group exercise and then discussed in a plenary session.

- Exercise A2 ("Our external context") can be used to develop an under-standing of the external threats and opportunities facing the organization. The questionnaire is completed by two different groups and then discussed in a plenary session. It can also be completed as an individual exercise.

- Exercise A3 ("Dreaming about the future") was designed to create a vision for the organization. The exercise works well with small groups, which then get together to share their ideas.

- Exercise A4 ("Beginning to bridge the gaps") is a group discussion that is used as a follow-up to Exercise A3.

EXERCISE A1

WHO IS XYZ? WHAT ARE THE STRENGTHS AND WEAKNESSES OF OUR INTERNAL ENVIRONMENT?

Purpose

To develop a common understanding of the five major strengths and weaknesses of XYZ.

Instructions

Part 1 (10 minutes)

- On your own, read the following list of elements that many organizations perceive as their strengths or weaknesses (see "Key-areas list," below). This is not a complete list and you may identify other strengths or weaknesses.
- As you read the list, ask yourself "Is XYZ particularly strong or weak in this area?"
- Write down XYZ's five major strengths and five major weaknesses.

Part 2 (30 minutes)

- Form a group with four other people.
- Share your lists and develop one common list of five strengths and five weaknesses.
- Write your final list on a flip chart.

Part 3 (the whole group)

- Review the team lists.
- Vote on the top five key areas.

Key-areas list

- Leadership (management culture, setting directions, supporting resource development, ensuring tasks are done)
- Identity (knowing who we are and what we are good at)
- Mission
- Organizational culture (attitudes about work, values, beliefs, underlying norms)
- Incentive and reward systems
- Governance (legal framework, decision-making process, representation on the Board of Directors, methods for setting directions)

- Organizational structure (roles and responsibilities, coordinating systems, authority structures)
- Niche recognition (understanding of uniqueness, areas of expertise)
- Staff
- Management of infrastructure (equipment, maintenance systems, choice of location)
- Financial systems (planning, managing, and monitoring cash flow)
- Fundraising capacities
- Communicating about the organization with our stakeholders
- Partnerships (types, numbers, cost–benefits, etc.)
- Networks (types, nature, utility, coordination, follow-up processes)
- Human-resource policy
- Career management
- Equity
- Compensation and reward
- Dedication and loyalty of our staff
- Expertise and quality of our staff
- Planning mechanisms (identifying needs, looking at alternatives, setting objectives, etc.)
- Problem-solving and decision-making (defining problems, gathering data, creating alternatives, monitoring decisions)
- Monitoring and evaluation (generating data, tracking progress, making judgments about performance)
- Skills and expertise in projects undertaken
- Building sustainable projects for community and Aboriginal groups
- Providing good value for money
- Relationships with beneficiaries
- Other (please list)

XYZ'S MAJOR STRENGTHS	XYZ'S MAJOR WEAKNESSES
1.	1.
2.	2.
3.	3.
4.	4.
5.	5.

EXERCISE A2
OUR EXTERNAL CONTEXT

Purpose

To understand the context within which XYZ is operating.

Instructions

Working in two groups, identify the major external threats and opportunities that have the biggest potential impacts on XYZ. Use the following list of elements that can positively or negatively affect an organization such as XYZ as a guide. You may identify other elements.

EXTERNAL FACTORS THAT MAY AFFECT XYZ	THREAT	OPPORTUNITY	NO MAJOR EFFECT
Support from member countries			
Support from host country			
Support from international funders			
Reliance of our organization on a few donors			
Collaborating institutions' support for XYZ's work			
XYZ's willingness to use electronic technology in its work			
Gap between XYZ's proclamation of support and its actions			
National attitudes toward regional cooperation			
National values for sharing with other countries in the region			
Policies of international bodies			
National leaders' desire to know about the impacts of XYZ			
Competition from other organizations doing similar work			
Demand for the type of services XYZ offers			
International demand for expertise in integrated rural development			
Reputation of the organization			
Disenchantment of donors with funding international bodies			
Disparities among members in the region, such as language or culture			
Link institutions' satisfaction with services			
External groups' lack of understanding of the target beneficiaries of XYZ			

EXERCISE A3
DREAMING ABOUT THE FUTURE

Purpose

To create a vision of XYZ as it will be in 3–5 years.

Instructions

Part 1 (20 minutes)

The year is 2001. You are a staff member of XYZ, and you have been asked to make a presentation about XYZ to a potential donor or link institution.

Working in a group of five, develop a 5–10 minute presentation. Your presentation should include

- A mission statement for XYZ
- A set of clients
- A set of donors and collaborators
- A description of your biggest success
- A description of what makes XYZ different

Part 2

- Write the main points of the presentation on a flip chart.
- Select a member of your group to make the actual presentation.

Part 3 (plenary)

- Make the presentation to the main group.

EXERCISE A4
BEGINNING TO BRIDGE THE GAPS

Purpose

To begin to make the vision for XYZ a reality.

Instructions

With the whole group, take 30 minutes to identify and discuss the following topics:

- The major gaps between XYZ's present situation and the vision created in Exercise A3
- The major areas in which XYZ needs to work to bridge the gaps.

THE AUTHORS

Charles Lusthaus, PhD, is an Associate Professor in the Department of Administration and Policy Studies, McGill University, and a partner in Universalia Management Group. His expertise is in organizational theory and in institutional evaluation and change. Dr Lusthaus has more than 20 years of experience in organizational development and assessment and has published more than 30 articles on topics related to educational management and policy development. He is one of the authors of *Institutional Assessment: A Framework for Strengthening Organizational Capacity for* IDRC's *Research Partners* and has also made more than 50 presentations at conferences and workshops. Dr Lusthaus is the Faculty Advisor for the Centre for Educational Leadership, McGill University.

Marie-Hélène Adrien, PhD, is a partner in Universalia Management Group. She has extensive experience in institutional and organizational evaluation and change, both in Canada and internationally. She works with medium-sized organizations from the public and private sectors to build individual and organizational capacities in response to organizational change: changing external context, diversified work force, emerging new training requirements, organizational restructuring, and changing stakeholder needs. She is one of the authors of *Évaluation institutionelle: cadre pour le renforcement des organizations partenaires du* CRDI. Her PhD and an MEd are from McGill University.

Gary Anderson, EdD, is an international authority on evaluation, education, and policy research and specializes in research studies and methodology. With more than 20 years experience in the field, he has designed, monitored, and evaluated education and training programs and has developed methodologies and frameworks for organizational development and analysis. He is the author of *Fundamentals of Educational Research* (2nd edition). Dr Anderson was the chair of the Department of Administration and Policy Studies, McGill University from 1985 to 1995. His BSc and MA are from McGill University, and he has a PhD in education from Harvard. He is a founding member and the president of Universalia Management Group.

Fred Carden, PhD, is Senior Specialist in Evaluation at the International Development Research Centre (Canada). He has extensive experience in international development and has written in the areas of evaluation, international cooperation, and environmental management. He has taught and carried out research at York University, the Cooperative College of Tanzania, the Bandung Institute of Technology (Indonesia), and the University of Indonesia. He has a PhD from the Université de Montréal and a Masters in environmental studies from York University.

Contacting us

Send your comments to

Marie-Hélène Adrien
Universalia Management Group
5252 de Maisonneuve Ouest
Montréal, Quebec
Canada H4A 3S5
Tel: (514) 485-3565
Fax: (514) 485-3210
e-mail: mha@umg.ca

Fred Carden
International Development Research Centre
250 Albert Street
PO Box 8500
Ottawa, Ontario
Canada K1G 3H9
Tel: (613) 236-6163
Fax: (613) 563-0815
e-mail: evaluation@idrc.ca
as well as by IDRC's agents and distributors around the world.

The Institution

The International Development Research Centre (IDRC) is committed to building a sustainable and equitable world. IDRC funds developing-world researchers, thus enabling the people of the South to find their own solutions to their own problems. IDRC also maintains information networks and forges linkages that allow Canadians and their developing-world partners to benefit equally from a global sharing of knowledge. Through its actions, IDRC is helping others to help themselves.

The Publisher

IDRC Books publishes research results and scholarly studies on global and regional issues related to sustainable and equitable development. As a specialist in development literature, IDRC Books contributes to the body of knowledge on these issues to further the cause of global understanding and equity. IDRC publications are sold through its head office in Ottawa, Canada,